INSTITUTIONAL architecture

INSTITUTIONAL architecture

The Design of Health Care, Educational, Municipal and Justice Facilities

BY

PAUL SILVER AND DAVID MILES ZISKIND

Architecture & Interior Design Library

An Imprint of

PBC INTERNATIONAL, INC.

Distributor to the book trade in the United States and Canada
Rizzoli International Publications Inc.
300 Park Avenue South
New York, NY 10010

Distributor to the art trade in the United States and Canada
PBC International, Inc.
One School Street
Glen Cove, NY 11542

Distributor throughout the rest of the world
Hearst Books International
1350 Avenue of the Americas
New York, NY 10019

LIBRARY OF CONGRESS
CATALOGING–IN–PUBLICATION DATA

Silver, Paul.
    Institutional architecture : the design of health care,
    educational, municipal, and justice facilities /
    Paul Silver, David Miles Ziskind.
        p.   cm. -- (Architecture & interior design library)
    Includes index.
    ISBN 0–86636–199–5   (international version ISBN 0-86636-295-9)
    1. Public buildings.
    2. Architecture, Modern--20th century.
    3. Architecture--Human factors.   I. Ziskind, David
    Miles. II. Title. III. Series.
NA4170.S48   1993
725--dc20   93–14868
                                                      CIP

CAVEAT– Information in this text is believed accurate, and will
pose no problem for the student or casual reader. However, the
author was often constrained by information contained in signed
release forms, information that could have been in error or not
included at all. Any misinformation (or lack of information) is
the result of failure in these attestations. The author has done
whatever is possible to insure accuracy.

Design by Eric Goodman

Color separation, printing and binding by
Toppan Printing Co. (H.K.) Ltd. Hong Kong

Printed in China

10 9 8 7 6 5 4 3 2 1

TABLE OF CONTENTS

FOREWORD

This book covers a wide range of building types from long term care centers to prisons. Most of my experience has been with the latter. However, the issues that emerge in designing correctional architecture go to the heart of the purpose of this book, of providing a measure of the potential for architects to create pleasing and humane environments - even for those who frighten and anger us.

Some years ago a colleague in corrections wrote a book, The New Red Barn, in which he contended that a first class prison could be operated out of an unlikely structure - even an old red barn. His notion was that what goes on within the building's walls is more than the architecture.

He was correct in his assertion that the major determinants of a first class correctional institution are the calibre of its leadership and staff, and the richness of the programs offered to inmates. But the compatibility of the physical plan with the activity it houses is not to be given short shrift when looking for ways to help achieve the goals of the enterprise. The exterior architecture can be a foreboding edifice as is the fortress type prison whose purpose must be to frighten would-be criminals. The old "Jimmy Cagney" prison, with its cavernous spaces, imposing cells and impersonal architecture presents a tough challenge to the enterprising warden who is intent on administering a safe and wholesome environment. Indeed, the physical plant often ends up stipulating how business will be done on several fronts.

The good building design ensures a secure institution, permits staff to be deployed efficiently, supports desirable group sizes, staves off the debilitating effects of limiting inmate activity, and avoids obtrusive surveillance that contributes to a dehumanizing environment. The exterior architecture can blend into surroundings, and even be accessible to the public, as is the jail embedded in a hill in St. Paul, Minnesota, which has a roof that provides a public garden.

With this in mind, when I served as Minnesota's corrections commissioner, we prepared an extensive design program for a maximum security prison - one that would be escape proof while affording a high level of variety and flexibility within its walls. Working from the hefty program prescription we prepared, Paul Silver designed what today is probably the world's most secure prison, located near Oak Park Heights, Minnesota. It is also a facility that provides spaces of human scale, opportunities for privacy, and the capability of implementing a wide range of options. Because it recedes into a hillside, it is unobtrusive to its neighbors.

In this book, INSTITUTIONAL ARCHITECTURE, Mr. Silver and Mr. Ziskind have assembled a collection of creative solutions to common architectural requirements. The authors communicate the important truth that with the same resources and with careful planning and skillful designing, an effective, efficient and pleasing structure can be constructed. INSTITUTIONAL ARCHITECTURE presents design options that are effective in function and form, and that can stand the test of time. One more thing, lest it is forgotten - well planned and poorly planned buildings have a feature in common - they will both endure for decades.

Kenneth F. Schoen
DIRECTOR
The Edna McConnell Clark Foundation
July 1993

The rise of the Modern Movement in architecture, almost a century ago, brought with it the unique notion that the world had reached such a degree of homogeneity that it was possible to postulate a singular style, and a singular set of design principles, which would cover every evolving culture.

This may very well have been the last manifestation of the European idea of colonialism, because to a very great extent it based its universality on the fact that the underlying force that drove the style was the implied consequence of worldwide industrialization.

The style, which has come to be known as the International Style, brought with it various postulates, with that of Mies van der Rohe's probably being the most universally believed. His view was that industrialization implied a specific physical design vocabulary and that vocabulary applied uniformly to all building types, quite independent of their function. This view held because all modern buildings drew their materials and systems from the pool of contemporary industrial product, which defined this design vocabulary.

Unfortunately for this "theory" the facts were of a different nature. The style, trapped in its minimalist aesthetic, simply lacked the capacity to sustain the richness of variety that could not be ignored as a necessary human interest. While it took several decades to exhaust these limitations, the term of the International Style, in the context of historical periods, has been a relatively short one.

The resulting declines of the style brought with it the realization that an enormous vacuum was created, seeking to be filled by another all encompassing theory of architecture. But this has not occurred, and what we have moved to is the recognition of the diversity of views, with many styles co-habitating in the same setting.

The disappearance of a singular theory has probably been felt most strongly by those building types that found the dictums of the International Style the most problematic to translate from theory into fact and where there was little cultural pressure to retain pre-style models, as it was in residential design. The building types that struggled the most against such rigid demands for uniformity of style and expression included many institutional and public structures, from hospitals to prisons, from nursing homes to courthouses.

What arose in this diversified design environment, represented in its architecture a wide range of eclectic views, all co-existing in a tenuous relationship, with each acting as if it was alone correct and waiting for the sorting out to confirm the universality of that point of view. In the meantime, we are required to go on, and the products of this current effort will remain with us for many a generation. It is with this awareness that we undertook this book. In essence, we are of the conviction that there is much that is good about some buildings that are being designed today, particularly in the areas where the minimalism of the International Style has had the greatest difficulty in establishing itself as truly appropriate.

In selecting projects for this volume we, therefore, chose to concentrate on those building types that have presented the greatest opportunity for designers to develop a unique and individual expression, while displaying that alternate design approaches could produce both wonderful and functional architecture.

All the projects that we have selected have aspects in common, and that is the facts that they are institutional and public structures, whose designs are often significantly influenced by the limitations of money and public attitudes. Clearly, only a very small part of the public holds an interest in what a prison environment is like, or how we care for the sick and needy. Yet, as architects we can never abandon our belief that every part of the built environment must be designed with the same degree of respect for its aesthetics, whether the subject of a design is a prison or a bus depot.

INTRODUCTION

We have organized the selected projects into a limited number of categories and included in each category designs of different perspectives. The projects, therefore, show differing points of view about the same design problem in different settings or in different community perspectives. However, in each case the projects demonstrate it is possible to achieve a quality of environment with significantly differing aesthetics.

Over the last thirty years we have observed the changes that have come to the once-certain principles of contemporary architecture and have recognized that much of what has changed has done little to improve our commitment to the simple humanist principle that architects should regard every building built as a design opportunity to produce an environment that elevates and delights all who use it.

This is particularly true of those building types that we tend to regard as strictly utilitarian and, therefore, simply not worthy of investing significant amounts of our limited resources or to apply our most creative efforts. We have always regarded this as a sorry commentary on our values. It is, therefore, satisfying to have the opportunity to demonstrate that there are those professionals among us who have chosen to work in building types and project areas which have long felt a lack of interest from the more widely recognized professionals whose reputations are built on the quality of their visual design.

It is also, and probably more significantly true that much of this work shows a sensitivity and awareness about the importance of design, and a thorough commitment to achieving quality in a challenging and not always supportive environment.

As we reach the end of a difficult and often unstable century, we are at a unique crossroads between an established architectural style that attempted to bring universal order to the design of buildings and the diversity of many different points of view. We are clearly without the tools to decide on the various options. It is also clear that there may not be such a universal option and we must, therefore, be content to live in a heterogeneous design world.

In such a world we are called upon to design our environment with a reverence for more fundamental principles which emphasize the quality of life while permitting diverse points of view on matters of form and detail. It is hoped that the content of this volume will help show such a balance.

When we undertook this book we realized at the start that gathering up many projects which we felt were needed to demonstrate that the quality of design need not be sacrificed to the demands of utilitarianism and the pragmatic limitation imposed by difficult budgets, was not going to be an easy task. We were fortunate to have Shaun Draper, who has worked diligently with us during the past year on this project. Her dedication to this book has helped see it through fruition.

In writing a book of this type it is important to have a point of view. We have always believed that the quality of architecture rises out of an understanding of human needs and desires and is not a remote or abstract art form having the elegance of mathematical formuli. Rather, it is more a part of the world of feelings with all its imprecision and unpredictability. It is for this reason we have chosen to use projects which are sometimes at variance with one school of thought or another but clearly possess the capacity to arouse emotions and stir interest.

We wish to thank all those architects, who by their works and their photographs have given us the means to demonstrate the diversity of contemporary design and the potential of producing exemplary architecture under the most limiting of circumstances.

HEALTH-RELATED FACILITIES

It appears that the more technologically sophisticated a design problem is, the more likely it is that the resulting design will be substantially devoid of aesthetic merit. The challenges of function have historically worked against the creation of an environment where the quality of the facility rises above mere workability.

It is particularly true of hospitals and nursing homes where the pragmatism of America has compelled the designer to seek workability over the aesthetic merits of a solution.

Because it takes so much technical knowledge to properly design and execute health-related facilities there always has to be a strong emphasis on workability; sometimes, however, the design created in specific instances demonstrates that it is possible to achieve both functionality and an aesthetic solution.

The demand for technological features in the design of a health-related facility is going to increase with the passing years. The tendency to build larger and larger facilities with more and more high technology will go on unabated.

It is because of this factor, alone, that the design of a health-related facility with significant aesthetic quality, leads to the need to acknowledge the importance of visual design even in such building types.

The projects that are good show a clear set of similarities. Those similarities show a real sense of homogeneity in the designs, have a self-contained look and seem whole within a large context.

Most health-related and community facilities are packed into an existing urban, or even sub-urban, infrastructure so that they often tend to overwhelm an existing complex or simply look alien in their setting, but the visual anthology of work shown in this chapter is all exemplary for the way in which it relates to existing physical settings, be it a park or a narrow urban street.

MOUNT SINAI MEDICAL CENTER-MRI ADDITION

Miami Beach, Florida

Modern technology produces both wonderful and frightening consequences. More often than not, the two can develop from the same technology. While in many cases the fears of undesirable consequences are justified in serious unwanted effects upon man and our environment, sometimes the fear is merely the result of associations.

The modern development of magnetic resonance images (MRI) has probably represented the most important diagnostic "tool" development since the x-ray. But unlike the x-ray its procedures are far more elaborate, the hardware far more intimidating and the requirements for its use more specialized. All of this lead to the need to recognize that patients are likely to have unjustified fears about the procedure, particularly if they also fear to discover hidden medical problems they may not be emotionally prepared to deal with.

Because of these factors, the design of a facility specifically dedicated to house MRI systems raises the issue of the quality and character of the environment to a higher plain than conventional examination or testing facilities.

Clearly, this facility was conceived to do everything possible to tell the patient that the setting for their examination is not merely comfortable but visually delightful, both day and night, and the interior inviting to be in despite one's reason. The exterior is expressive of the internal organization of the plan around the two testing units, and the entry walk and landscaping create a wonderful feeling of accessibility.

PROJECT
Mount Sinai Medical Center-MRI Addition
Miami Beach, FL

CLIENT
Mount Sinai Medical Center
Miami Beach, FL

ARCHITECTS
The Gruzen Partnership
Project Directors: Paul Silver, FAIA and David Miles
Ziskind, AIA
Silver & Ziskind
New York, NY

PHOTOGRAPHER
Mel Victor
Miami, FL

COVE'S EDGE LONG TERM CARE CENTER

Damariscotta, Maine

In an environment which requires the cooperation of individuals who are limited in their mobility and whose demand for services can compromise the quality of the living environment, it is a substantial accomplishment to produce a sense of "home-ness" and residential quietude that reinforce the importance, the feeling and the appearance of the physical environment.

Cove's Edge achieves much of these qualities with its modest scale and very residential character. It never overwhelms the eye or threatens a loss of visual delight.

To attain a warm, non-institutional environment at Cove's Edge, light was introduced through five cupola-topped skylights that brighten the center's entrance lobby and two main patient wings. The cupolas, constructed of wood frame and lattice, echo traditional Maine architecture and also create an appealing lighting patchwork inside the facility.

A hometown concept is achieved in the creation of two main patient corridors that function as a "Main Street." The corridors are carpeted and unusually wide to allow space for a sitting area outside patient rooms. The corridors converge at the central nursing station—the "town square" and hub of activity, positioned just off the entrance lobby.

The innovative design characteristics of Cove's Edge have created an affable environment that is beneficial to its residents while also providing a productive and practical environment for the staff.

PROJECT
Cove's Edge Long Term Care Center
Damariscotta, ME

CLIENT
Miles Development Foundation
Damariscotta, ME

ARCHITECT
Rothman Rothman Heineman Architects Inc.
Boston, MA

PHOTOGRAPHER
Steve Rosenthal (Courtesy of Rothman Rothman
Heineman Architects Inc.)
Auburndale, MA

DAVID GRANT MEDICAL CENTER TRAVIS AIR FORCE BASE

Fairfield, California

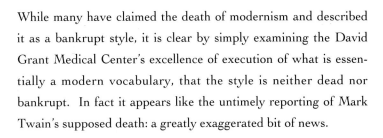

While many have claimed the death of modernism and described it as a bankrupt style, it is clear by simply examining the David Grant Medical Center's excellence of execution of what is essentially a modern vocabulary, that the style is neither dead nor bankrupt. In fact it appears like the untimely reporting of Mark Twain's supposed death: a greatly exaggerated bit of news.

The design for a client like the United States Air Force demonstrates the fact that such an institution can rise so high to a level of commitment to quality, that it can represent a standard for others.

The color and forms of the building have both the variety and scale, so much a feature of California's architecture. Set in the dry regions around the Sacramento River delta where the grass turns golden, the design reflects the soothing earth colors indigenous to the area.

The interior carries forward the exterior formal expression, and the detail and color preserve the sense of a continuity between the exterior world of forms and colors and the interior environment of space and surface.

Given its considerable size, over 800,000 square feet, and the compulsion to enclose such masses into large monolithic blocks, it is a significant demonstration that it is possible to achieve functionality and scale, efficiency and humanity within large and complex projects.

PROJECT
David Grant Medical Center
Travis Air Force Base
Fairfield, CA

CLIENT
United States Air Force
Travis Air Force Base
Fairfield, CA

ARCHITECT
NBBJ
Seattle, WA

PHOTOGRAPHER
Jane Lidz
San Francisco, CA

LAUREL RIDGE PSYCHIATRIC HOSPITAL

San Antonio, Texas

Psychiatric hospitals have represented one of the most neglected building types. Confronted with problems of extraordinary complexity and requiring inordinate technical sophistication by the designer, this building type has produced almost no exemplary examples which demonstrate a quality of environmental design.

Laurel Ridge represents a rare exception. This facility illustrates a character and sensitivity that is the mark of humane and architectural superior solutions.

With a vernacular reminiscent of Mission Style it creates a quiet but varied series of spaces formed by walls of arcades that define the space without displaying the buildings they hide. This quality is further enhanced by the repetition of simple elements like the arch, pitched tile roofs and stucco exterior wall finish.

This facility clearly produces a variety of closely related spaces from a simple but visually delightful group of elements. Therefore, the real source of its design strength lies in the creation of a setting which is both serene and harmonious.

PROJECT
Laurel Ridge Psychiatric Hospital
San Antonio, TX

CLIENT
Laurel Ridge Psychiatric Hospital
San Antonio, TX

ARCHITECT
HKS, Inc.
Dallas, TX

PHOTOGRAPHER
Greg Hursley
Austin, TX

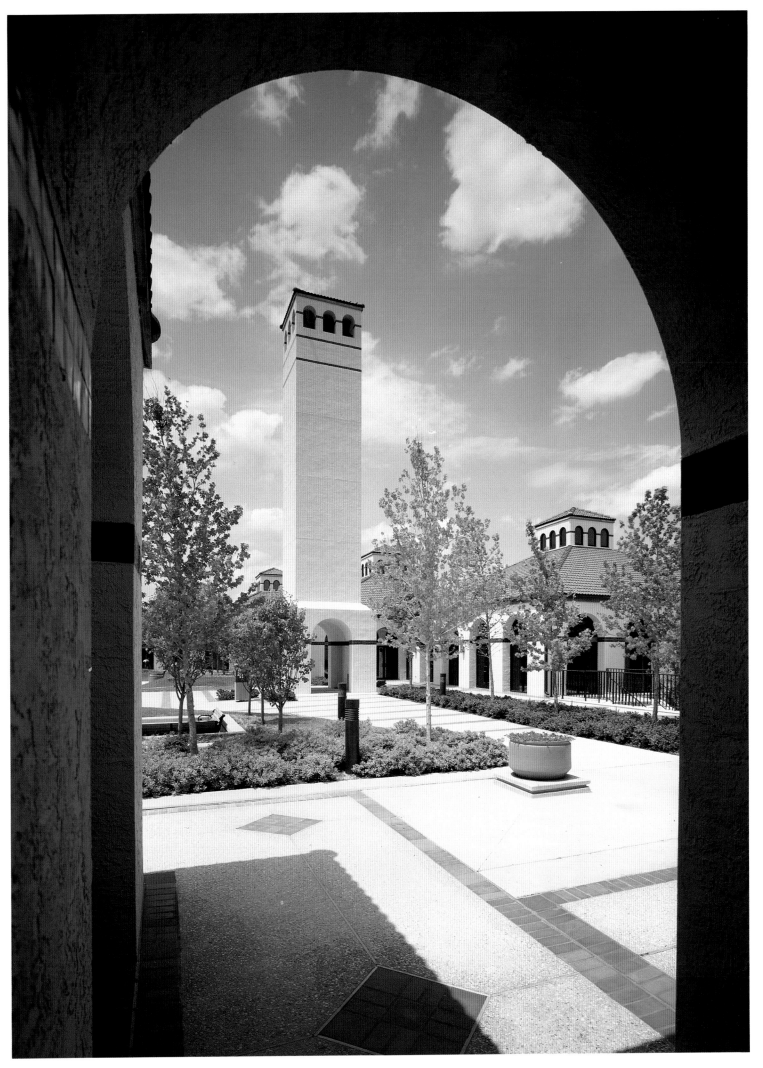

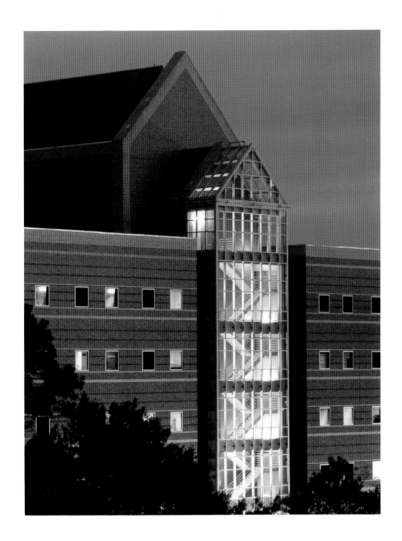

BEN TAUB REPLACEMENT HOSPITAL

Houston, Texas

Houston is a city known for the exceptional quality of its medical facilities, particularly the world renowned Texas Medical Center. As a building set within an existing complex, the Ben Taub Replacement Hospital replaces a previous facility located on the same site.

Thus as a phoenix, it rises above its former self as a totally new entity, conceived in a style and character of this time. Its use of a uniquely shaped nursing unit, generates a large mega-block which is relieved by the use of a multi-story atrium of glass and steel, filled with light and a sense of drama.

The stated design goal of the architect was to "upgrade and enhance one of the most advanced full-service general acute care facilities while offering quality design with maximum flexibility, as well as make a statement expressing the owner's commitment to provide the indigent with excellence in healthcare; and to respond to the unique character of the neighboring university campus."

What is interesting about the design is its relationship to its user population, which includes indigents. Surely the character of this environment will not be seen as hostile to those who cannot afford the expense of private medical care. Ben Taub Replacement Hospital successfully communicates a non-hostile environment to its users.

PROJECT
Ben Taub Replacement Hospital
Houston, TX

CLIENT
Harris County Hospital District
Houston, TX

ARCHITECT
CRSS Architects, Inc.
Houston, TX
in joint venture with
Llewellyn Davies-Sahni, Inc.
Houston, TX

PHOTOGRAPHER
Joe C. Aker
Houston, TX

ST. CATHERINE'S VILLAGE

Madison, Mississippi

Despite the mood of our highly pragmatic society to condemn romanticism, there appears to be little reason in fact to deny that some of the most wonderful works of art arose from that now discredited style. Underlying all of the romantic art of the late last century was an intense commitment to generating strong moods that richly recall the past, often based on idealized recollections.

It may be for the elderly with their many years of recollections, an even more fundamental capacity. It is, therefore, a seemingly appropriate design idea to consider creating a truly romantic setting. It is also clear that St. Catherine's Village, a retirement community for the elderly does it in a superb manner while still creating gracious lifestyles for three diverse levels of living: independent, assisted and full nursing care.

Set along the edge of a lake it is reminiscent of the scale of Dutch and German medieval farm villages with a scale that is so comfortable as to be magical. The forms and massing are pleasantly homogeneous but never dull; in fact, they are full of small but significant variations around a theme such as the tiled pitched roofs and curved end walls of glass.

While the exterior is surely a romantic setting the interior never loses its residential tranquility. A feeling of "home-ness", of coming home to a safe and comfortable setting is reinforced with every detail, be it the dining rooms ceiling beams, the walls of glass doors or the low key lighting throughout.

PROJECT
St. Catherine's Village
Madison, MS

CLIENT
Community Health Service
St. Dominic's Inc. (A subsidiary of St. Dominic's
Health Services, Inc.)
Jackson, MS

ARCHITECT
Cooke Douglass Farr Lemons/Ltd.
Jackson, MS
Consultant
Samuel Mockbee, FAIA
Auburn, AL

PHOTOGRAPHER
John O'Hagan
Birmingham, AL

CENTRAL WASHINGTON HOSPITAL-EMERGENCY AND AMBULATORY SURGERY ADDITION

Wenatchee, Washington

At first glance, there seem to be features of this project which remind the viewer of post-modern forms. The design is in the best sense classical modernism at its very best. The "punch" wall entry with its cantilevered marquee provides a powerful visual cue, while the use of bright colors draws the eye to this central point of entry.

There is a pleasant consistency between what happens on the exterior of the building and what goes on inside. The spaces, their forms and textures are directly related to those used on the exterior, and the scale and placement of openings recalls that relationship.

As a hospital it represents a significant divergence from the strictly separated exterior design character and interior design feeling that is the most obvious hallmark of most hospitals. It is almost an axiom of this building type that the internal working of the hospital so prescribes a design character that the only aesthetic "design" role the architect has is in his treatment of the exterior. It is important to recognize that this need not be so, and, in fact, it is possible to remain committed to a functional design while still creating an overall facility environment that brings harmony to the relationship between the world of the building's exterior and the world of its interior.

PROJECT
Central Washington Hospital-Emergency
and Ambulatory Surgery Addition
Wenatchee, WA

CLIENT
Central Washington Hospital
Wenatchee, WA

ARCHITECT
NBBJ
Seattle, WA

PHOTOGRAPHER
Paul Warchol
New York, NY

BAPTIST HOSPITAL OF MIAMI-LAKE PAVILION ADDITION

Miami, Florida

The Baptist Hospital of Miami is a multi-facility grouping, which has grown over the years by the addition of pavilions. The Lake Pavilion Addition is rich with the recall of Italian Renaissance detail, while not being blindly imitative. Whether it is the entrance porte cochere or the campanile water tower, the enclosing elements borrow richly from Renaissance forms.

One of the most delightful features of the design, both in the exterior and the interior, is the use of strong, highly relieved horizontal and vertical color bandings, sometimes alone and sometimes in groupings of three. These bands provide a unifying visual device connecting spaces often of divergent form and varied detail.

A pleasant aspect of the design is the simple natural landscaping, with tall and slender palm trees set in the center of the outdoor courtyards. The courtyards are so reminiscent of the Italian patio house in scale and detail, that it is quite easy to imagine this space to be merely one of several interior outdoor spaces of someone's private villa. This is true despite the size and scale of the entire hospital complex.

The materials and finishes, along with the pale pastel colors are a common vocabulary of this region and are used in a manner that is quieting and restrained. The resulting design is one of visual comfort and a restful mood.

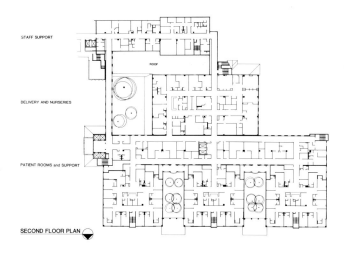

STAFF SUPPORT

ROOF

DELIVERY AND NURSERIES

PATIENT ROOMS and SUPPORT

SECOND FLOOR PLAN

PROJECT
Baptist Hospital of Miami-Lake Pavilion Addition
Miami, FL

CLIENT
Baptist Hospital of Miami
Miami, FL

ARCHITECT
TRO\The Ritchie Organization
Sarasota, FL

PHOTOGRAPHERS
John Gillan
Miami, FL   (all others)

Robert E. Mikrut
Newport, RI   (page 41)

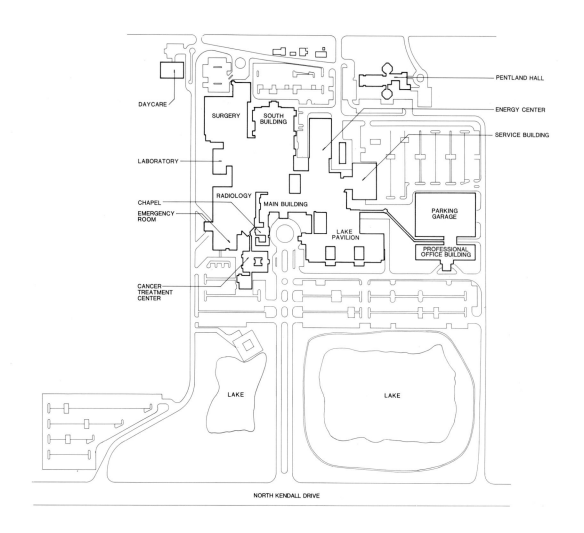

DAYCARE

SURGERY

SOUTH BUILDING

LABORATORY

CHAPEL

RADIOLOGY

MAIN BUILDING

EMERGENCY ROOM

LAKE PAVILION

CANCER TREATMENT CENTER

PENTLAND HALL

ENERGY CENTER

SERVICE BUILDING

PARKING GARAGE

PROFESSIONAL OFFICE BUILDING

LAKE

LAKE

NORTH KENDALL DRIVE

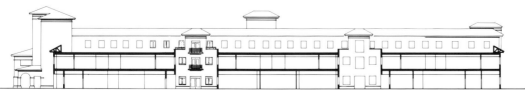

THE WOMEN'S PAVILION AT GWINNETT MEDICAL CENTER
Lawrenceville, Georgia

It is always problematic to add major new components onto an existing hospital facility grouping. All too often, the complex becomes a potpourri of conflicting styles as each new component screams for recognition as the central or "best" design structure on the site.

The addition of a Women's Pavilion at Gwinnett Medical Center could easily have resulted in such a mish-mosh of design. The result, however, is one of harmonious compatibility even though the scale and treatment of the new pavilion differs in many important ways from that of the existing structures.

The treatment of the surfaces may be different, but the basic vocabulary of materials and the scale of detail, like window proportions, and general pattern, relate to the existing structure.

The interior of this facility is clearly designed around an acute awareness of the special needs of the users. This is not merely "functional" utilitarianism, rather it appears to begin with the recognition of need for comforting and quieting, homey qualities only modified to the extent that medical requirements demand. Even then, the medical features of these environments are made as unobtrusive as possible. There is a quiet serenity about this environment, which seems so appropriate to its special function.

PROJECT
The Women's Pavilion at Gwinnett Medical Center
Lawrenceville, GA

CLIENT
Gwinnett Medical Center
Lawrenceville, GA

ARCHITECT
Nix, Mann and Associates, Inc.
Atlanta, GA

PHOTOGRAPHER
Timothy Hursley
Little Rock, AR

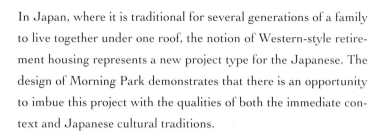

MORNING PARK CHIKARAMACHI RETIREMENT COMMUNITY

Nagoya, Japan

In Japan, where it is traditional for several generations of a family to live together under one roof, the notion of Western-style retirement housing represents a new project type for the Japanese. The design of Morning Park demonstrates that there is an opportunity to imbue this project with the qualities of both the immediate context and Japanese cultural traditions.

The creation of a gathering place to promote social interaction among residents is the project's primary organizing feature. A courtyard serves as the symbol of a cohesive community and draws residents out of their apartments with al fresco dining, a multi-purpose pavilion atop a waterfall and reflecting pond, and garden areas.

The setting of this building, within a dense urban context could easily have produced a chaotic and confused array of parts. The design has, however, shown an extraordinary sensitivity to scale and detail within a highly organized and even overall symmetrical form. What is most outstanding is the facility's delicacy of detail, its fineness of line which significantly reduces the scale and provides a hospitable, non-institutional quality almost always lacking in this building type.

PROJECT
Morning Park Chikaramachi Retirement Community
Nagoya, Japan

CLIENT
Human Life Services
Tokyo, Japan

ARCHITECT
Kaplan McLaughlin Diaz
San Francisco, CA
Associate Architect
Kajima Corp.
Nagoya, Japan

PHOTOGRAPHY
Shinkenchiku-Sha Co., LTD.
Tokyo, Japan

FLAGLER HOSPITAL
St. Augustine, Florida

Located in St. Augustine, the oldest city in this country, the Flagler Hospital is another representation of that difficult cross between strictly modern forms and the eclectic detail of earlier styles.

What is particularly interesting about this low rise sprawling facility is its excellent use of color and texture and the enormous variety without any loss of a sense of order and organization. The red columned upper portico and the aqua window bands in isolation would seem out of character but on the contrary, they add a richness of detail and restraint that results in a pleasant and inviting facade.

The interior spaces carry through some of the features of the exterior but, in an essential way, are different from the outside character. The interior, while heavily articulated, like the exterior wall surfaces, is extremely modest in scale with walls and columns detailed in a manner that almost consciously dramatizes largeness. Where the columns are large and horizontally banded and the interior borrowed lights framed in large mullion wall units as in the waiting areas, it is possible to see how the interior differs from the larger scale of the exterior.

It is so much a lost principal in these days of flat roofs, that the color, forms and texture of the pitched roof can contribute in an almost unmeasurable way to the sense of unity and order of a building complex with many and varied users and uses.

PROJECT
Flagler Hospital
St. Augustine. FL

CLIENT
Flagler Hospital
St. Augustine, FL

ARCHITECT
Hansen Lind Meyer
Orlando, FL

PHOTOGRAPHER
Phil Eschbach
Winter Park, FL

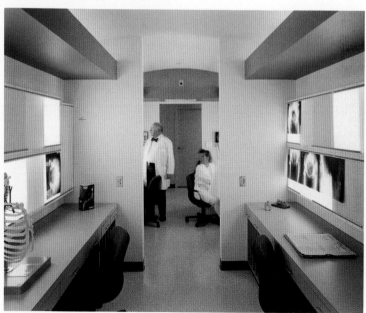

THE EMORY CLINIC- SPORTS MEDICINE & SPINAL INSTITUTE

Decatur, Georgia

Athletics has always implied a kind of rough vigor lacking in such other physical activities like dance. Therefore, it seems appropriate that a facility designed for physical medicine should be set in what looks like a purely functional setting made visually exciting, with the use of strong color contrasts. The details of the facility are quite simple and reasonably familiar, but what are special aspects of the design are both its use of color and the correctness of the mood created by the utilitarian design and the elevated levels of color.

One pleasant feature of the Emory Clinic design shows up in the large equipment room, where despite the clutter of equipment of all sorts and sizes the room remains a unified space bound together by a combination of colored spiral ductwork and round corrugated column covers.

There is no attempt to be subtle here, this is a world of rough and tumble athletics and the facility is not going to imply any need to be quiet or passive. The setting is in effect the color and the simple conventional architectural forms so common to the period, but the mood it conveys is bold and frankly "athletic" with the kind of ruggedness we would expect from athletes fighting back from an injury to regained health and well-being.

PROJECT
The Emory Clinic-Sports Medicine & Spinal Institute
Decatur, GA

CLIENT
The Emory Clinic
Atlanta, GA

ARCHITECT
Nix, Mann and Associates, Inc.
Atlanta, GA

PHOTOGRAPHER
Tod Swiecichowski
Little Rock, AR

CALIFORNIA STATE
SCHOOL FOR THE BLIND

Fremont, California

As a design profession, almost entirely driven by the visual world, the designing of an environment for the blind presents double challenges. One is to respond to the special needs of the blind and the other is to provide a visually pleasing setting for the sighted.

California State School For The Blind is an extremely successful resolution of both of these goals and was designed to recreate an urban environment to enable students to understand and deal with experiences encountered in the "real" world. The design is organized into several sub-settings or distinct groupings, including a residential district, a classroom district and a town center. The resulting groupings form what is a condensed version of a town or village.

What is so delightful about this design is its wonderful use of strong sculptured forms, with brightly colored elements, from canopies to window frames to signage. This facility demonstrates that modern design concepts still have much vitality left.

PROJECT
California State School for the Blind
Fremont, CA

CLIENT
The State of California

ARCHITECT
Dworsky Associates
Los Angeles, CA

PHOTOGRAPHER
Jane Lidz
San Francisco, CA

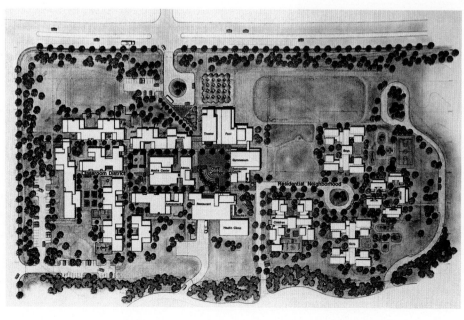

MINNEAPOLIS CHILDREN'S HOSPITAL

Minneapolis, Minnesota

As an audience for architectural environment, children have tended to be short changed by the lack of designs that respond to their unique needs and desires. All too often environments designed for children are either miniature adult worlds or over ornamented visually cluttered settings full of animated wallpapers and floor tiles. This seldom goes to the root of what children find pleasant, or for that matter inviting. Surely we have over the years developed a fairly good understanding that many of the qualities we relish about good environmental design as adults apply equally well to children, particularly when they are ill or away from familiar secure settings.

It is therefore of some importance to stress the role of color and lighting, of scale on detail in a children's environment as well as it would be in an adult setting. What is pleasant about the interior spaces at the Minneapolis Children's Medical Center is the use of color and detail which is subdued, but filled with small and visually prominent accents in the form of bands of color, edge trims of color and dropped soffits filled with bright indirect light sources making the environment modestly playful, serene at times and always unintimidating and non-institutional.

In one sense this dramatizes the fact that children are in some important ways no different from adults, but a close look at the interior architecture clearly shows an awareness of the need for a scale smaller than that associated with adult facilities. This in some sense, shows the effect of combining mood impacting features like color and texture with scale modulation to create a small-children's-world.

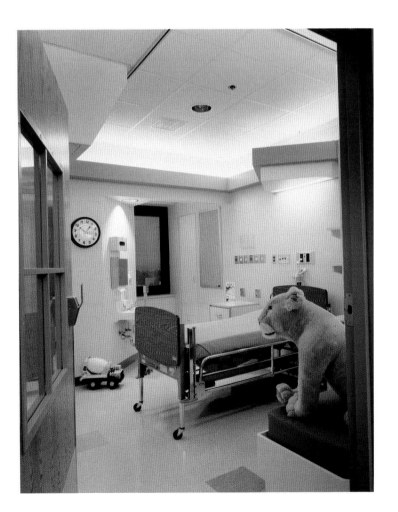

PROJECT
Minneapolis Children's Hospital
Minneapolis, MN

CLIENT
Lifespan, Inc.
Minneapolis, MN

ARCHITECT
Hansen Lind Meyer
Iowa City, IA

PHOTOGRAPHER
Phillip James
St. Paul, MN

VOLLUM INSTITUTE FOR ADVANCED BIOMEDICAL RESEARCH

Portland, Oregon

The more highly specialized and varied the spaces of a building's program gets, the more likely that the design will get confused and lack a central focus. This is particularly true of multi-story projects. Despite the tremendous variety of functions and varied spatial demands, the Vollum Institute has an exceptional sense of unity combined with a highly successful overall expression. The facade is a fine blending of form and surface treatment.

The gently curved exterior wall, combined with window pattern and wall texture, results in one of the best new urban building facades to be found today. But it is the interior, with its warm collegial quality that brings this design far beyond mere competence.

The interior, be it a library or a laboratory is pleasant and well exceeds the general accepted standard. It would seem to be a wonderful work setting that continually, by its very character, reinforces the importance of this facility's research functions and gives lasting dignity to those works. Clearly, it also states that people, and their strictly human needs, are exceedingly important.

It would not be fair to this project, to fail to mention its site treatment as well, which is consistent and supportive of the whole design. The "front yard" entry area steps and paving function as much as a part of the building as does the facade. There is a pleasant unity to this building, often not achievable in an urban context.

PROJECT
Vollum Institute for Advanced Biomedical Research
Portland, OR

CLIENT
Oregon Health Sciences University
Portland, OR

ARCHITECT
Zimmer Gunsul Frasca Partnership
Portland, OR

PHOTOGRAPHERS
Timothy Hursley
Little Rock, AR   (page 61 bottom, 63)

Strode Eckert Photographic
Portland, OR   (all others)

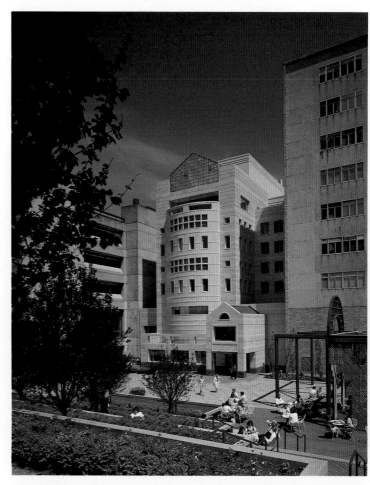

CHILDREN'S HOSPITAL AND HEALTH CENTER—NEW PATIENT PAVILION

San Diego, California

Simply as an architectural project, this effort would justify attention and appreciation. Aside from its difficult role in providing for the care and treatment of children, it possesses a formal quality that includes playful and varied geometries. There is a sense of novelty about the use of pitched roofs capped with "monitors" forms set against arched walls and pointed gables. The combination would almost imply clutter yet it is skillfully used here to give scale and articulation.

The clock tower does more than provide for the mounting of a clock, it is in essence the visual focus of the project calling out the entrance from a distance. The effect of all of these elements is faintly reminiscent of the delightful scale and aesthetic character of Dutch city residential design of the 16th and 17th centuries. While this is surely not intended as a literal recall, it does capture the essential feeling shared by both settings. It is a delight in small scale detail, articulating what could be large unadorned flat surfaces and a variety of roof lines to prevent the monotony of an endlessly repeated treatment from making the whole look like a massive singular structure.

The interior is an extension of this playfulness, reinforced in a number of features, including the multi-colored floor tile pattern and the points-of-light ceiling that gives a celestial-dome look to the corridors.

PROJECT
Children's Hospital and Health Center-New Patient Pavilion
San Diego, CA

CLIENT
Children's Hospital and Health Center
San Diego, CA

ARCHITECT
NBBJ
Seattle, WA

PHOTOGRAPHER
Hewitt/Garrison
San Diego, CA

JUSTICE FACILITIES

In the early 1960s, almost 200 years after the founding of the republic, the deplorable conditions of confinement in the jails and prisons throughout the land became enough a matter of public concern that it reached the level of a constitutional issue. The highest court of the land pronounced an unprecedented opinion that many of the existing facilities in this country represented, in effect, cruel and unusual punishment.

What was a history shattering ruling carried with it the implication that there would have to be substantial physical changes in these facilities. The resulting changes in the design of jails and prisons has been given the name "new generation." The first ten years of this period were driven almost entirely by the underlying constitutional issues of cruel and unusual punishment. But the years to follow continued on with the design principles developed at that time, altered only by the fact that the second phase of this new generation of designs was driven by a dramatic increase in rates of incarceration, and was, therefore, principally a response to overcrowding.

The development of more jail and prison facilities which responded to a growing inmate population brought with it greater demands on the other sectors of the criminal justice system. The result has been a significant increase in the need for police and court facilities. The response to this demand has only just begun to develop the new facilities to answer this need.

There is a considerable body of work that has been produced by architects in the last two decades in the areas of jail and prison design. Much of it is marked by the features that have become the hallmarks of contemporary design of this building type. What is probably the most distinguishing feature of contemporary jail and prison design is the restructuring of the inmate living areas into smaller units with a great many services being brought to the inmate to minimize the intra-facility movement.

What has happened to jails and prisons has to a similar extent happened to courthouses, i.e., the form of the building has changed in response to a new set of objectives. While the objectives in the case of jails and prisons were compliance with constitutional standards, the courts' objectives were to provide secure and efficient space in a high use volume environment. The resulting designs have taken on new formal features which make these newer courthouses different in significant ways. These differences manifest themselves in both a change in the physical arrangements of the spaces that make up a courthouse and in the configuration and layout of the courtroom itself.

We have chosen a number of courthouse buildings to include in this section that, by virtue of their designs, show how dramatically these new requirements drive the physical form of the modern courthouse in a direction quite unlike its traditional predecessors.

In effect, there are probably no building types that have undergone a more dramatic change than jails and prisons. And, there is probably no building type that has more compelling demands for new concepts than the courthouse, with its ever increasing demand for greater and greater security.

FEDERAL CORRECTIONAL INSTITUTE
Marianna, Florida

Within the vocabulary of correctional architecture's palette of materials are those common to our experience and those, when used appropriately, appear to be drawn from another context. It is for that reason we look upon some of the designs of the Federal Bureau of Prisons and respond with pleasant surprise at how they have been able to introduce glass and wood in extensive quantities into their new facilities without compromising their correctional objectives.

It is equally interesting to note that even when they have remained within the vocabulary of traditional materials they have successfully stimulated their design professionals to achieve both character and scale, a significant departure from the forms and expressions conventionally associated with prison architecture.

The Federal Correctional Institute of Marianna, Florida, is an example of how it is possible to take a more conventional vocabulary of materials and make use of them by blending and grouping to produce a facility that preserves the scale and humanity often not associated with hard masonry and concrete materials. In a sense, the Federal Bureau of Prisons has lead the way to new expressions to cloak the basic building forms that they have found to be the functional units of their operations.

PROJECT
Federal Correctional Institute
Marianna, FL

CLIENT
U.S. Department of Justice
Federal Bureau of Prisons
Washington, DC

ARCHITECT
Hansen Lind Meyer
Orlando, FL

PHOTOGRAPHER
Phil Eschbach
Winter Park, FL

BUCHANAN COUNTY/ ST. JOSEPH LAW ENFORCEMENT CENTER

St. Joseph, Missouri

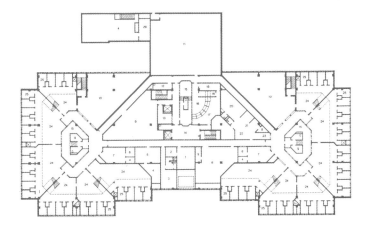

The exterior design of a combined law enforcement detention facility often poses diametrically opposed design problems — police tend to see the security of their operations as protection against intruders from outside, while detention is concerned with holding a population within. The Buchanan County Law Enforcement Center has treated the exterior as two interlocking masses or blocks with each expressing its difference in function.

The outer wall of the inmate areas consists of neatly fashioned concrete squares forming an interfacing of strip windows and vertical bands. This expression of block or cells emphasizes the hidden inner geometry in an interesting formal way without reducing it to a mundane pattern of slit windows and masonry joints.

The base of the building supporting these blocks consists of masonry walls which at times step up and down and run out beyond the face of the building anchoring the facility firmly to the site. The contrast of hard flat surfaces of the cell area and the darker articulated base of brick help to reinforce a sense of mass without developing a feeling of oppressive scale or monumentality.

A particularly interesting feature of the design is the circular window at the entrance which draws both the eye and light into the entry area.

PROJECT
Buchanan County/St. Joseph Law Enforcement Center
St. Joseph, MO

CLIENT
Buchanan County Board of County Commissioners
And the City of St. Joseph
St. Joseph, MO

ARCHITECT
Shaughnessy Fickel and Scott Architects Inc.
Kansas City, MO

PHOTOGRAPHER
Michael Christianer, AIA
Kansas City, MO

DOWNTOWN JUSTICE CENTER

Portland, Oregon

In our pragmatic age, when simplicity and bland efficiency are synonymous with quality, it is a mark of the fact that more spiritual values survive when a building is designed which makes as much of its environment as it does of its efficiency. The drama this design message conveys about the importance of public spaces revives a long neglected concept that public architecture should demonstrate the value of our institutions, their importance and their civic role. There is hardly a better example of that than the new Downtown Justice Center in Portland, Oregon.

Sited opposite a downtown park and opposite the well-known Portland Building designed by Michael Graves, it provides the combination of grandeur and sobriety with tasteful drama, so important to a courthouse.

The jail and police functions located on the upper floors are not compromised to meet the needs of the courtrooms below. In fact, in many ways, the jail design is fully respectful of all the contemporary goals and standards associated with detention facilities. While the balance of public spaces are modest in scale, they possess a serene dignity that is neither intimidating nor fanciful.

The design is a rare example of a carefully organized assemblage of related but significantly different functions, which produce an environment of special public value.

PROJECT
Downtown Justice Center
Portland, OR

CLIENT
Oregon Department of Transportation
Multnomah County
City of Portland, OR

ARCHITECT
Zimmer Gunsul Frasca Partnership
Portland, OR

PHOTOGRAPHERS
Ed Hershberger
Portland, OR   (page 75)

Timothy Hursley
Little Rock, AR   (all others)

Robert Reynolds
Portland, OR   (page 74 bottom)

DISTRICT OF COLUMBIA CORRECTIONAL AND TREATMENT FACILITY

Washington, District of Columbia

Frequently, an architect is called upon to design a building which has significantly new program functions. The District of Columbia's Correctional and Treatment Facility is such a project, being a correctional facility substantially committed to mental health and drug abuse treatment. It could have easily become the expression of a "conventional prison," but the architects chose to develop a design emphasizing a scale and spatiality characteristic of the surrounding community, and presenting an inviting face to the public. The buildings are arranged to form a spacious fore-court entrance shaded by a basque of trees providing scale, a sense of spatial depth and a texture to the setting.

Both internally and externally, the facility consists of a series of small architectural elements connected internally by an interior street that provides access to the various parts of the facility.

The housing units break away from the conventional correctional format of the day room surrounded by inmate rooms. Here, a cluster of individual sleeping rooms are grouped together and arranged so that the day space acts as a hub, of a hub and spoke management.

The design demonstrates how greatly varied functions can be integrated into a facility without producing an overwhelming and over-scaled structure.

PROJECT
District of Columbia Correctional and Treatment Facility
Washington, DC

CLIENT
District of Columbia
Department of Public Works
Washington, DC

ARCHITECT
Silver & Ziskind
New York, NY

PHOTOGRAPHER
Doug Brown
Alexandria, VA

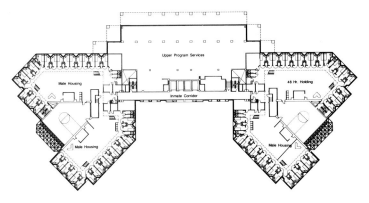

SUFFOLK COUNTY JAIL
Boston, Massachusetts

Located along the edge of the Charles River in Boston, Massachusetts, this detention center is set in a fabric of interesting roads and highways. The design of the facility could have easily been abandoned to these restrictions, but the concept developed sought and achieved a residential scale by sub-dividing the long facade into smaller, highly articulated elements. The modesty of the entrance and the use of material and details bring a certain sense of historical recall to the building without it being eclectic or imitative.

The pre-cast units used to form the windows clearly escape the look of the all too common narrow-prison window slits that have become the symbol of facilities for incarceration. By grouping the windows of two adjacent rooms together, the resulting effect is the impression of one large window. Security is still maintained by angling the windows at 90 degrees from its companion so that visual contact between the cells is avoided.

This project was developed in an innovative design-build competition and demonstrates that even under new or unusual design and construction strategies it is possible to achieve excellence.

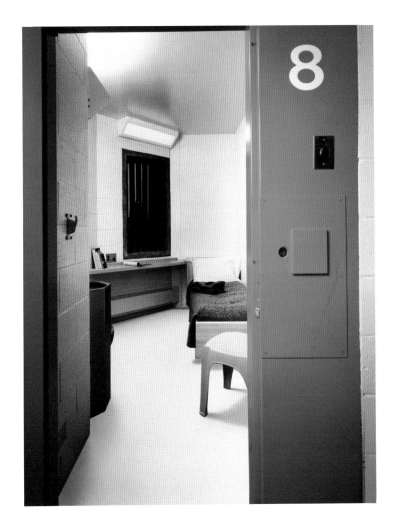

PROJECT
Suffolk County Jail
Boston, MA

CLIENT
Commonwealth of Massachusetts
Division of Capital Planning and Operations
Corrections Special Unit
Boston, MA

ARCHITECT
The Stubbins Associates, Inc.
Cambridge, MA
Associate Architect for Corrections
Voinovich-Monacelli Associates
Cambridge, MA

PHOTOGRAPHER
Edward Jacoby (Courtesy of the Stubbins Associates, Inc.)
Boston, MA

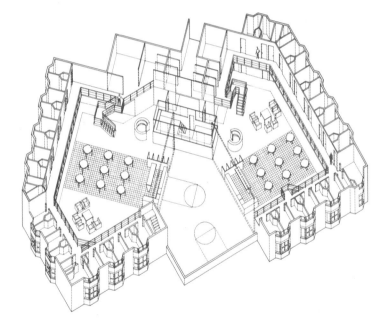

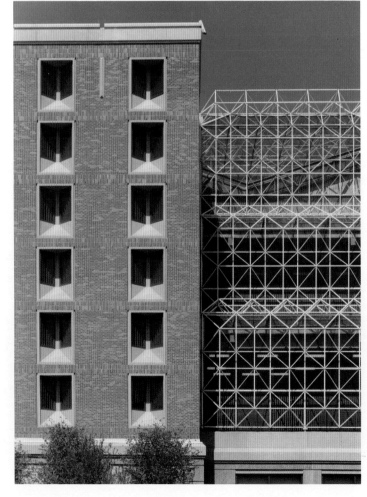

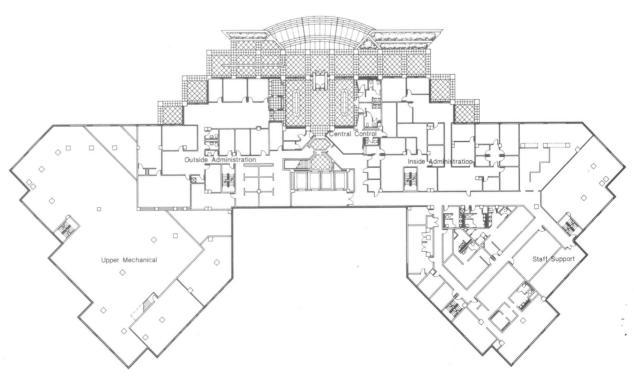

Outside Administration

Central Control

Inside Administration

Upper Mechanical

Staff Support

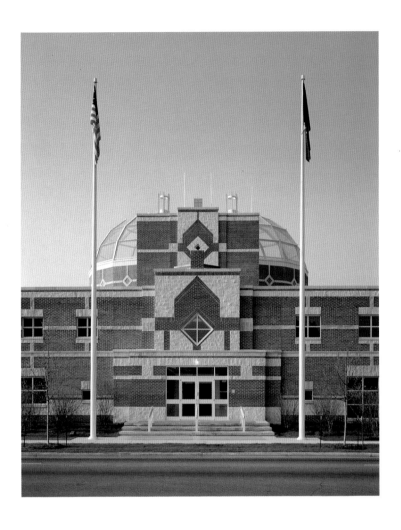

BARTHOLOMEW COUNTY JAIL
Columbus, Indiana

Columbus, Indiana, has over the last four decades become a living museum of contemporary American architecture. It is endowed with what is probably the greatest concentration of major architectural projects in any city of its size.

The leading architects of our time have found this community to be committed to a quality of environment which has made Columbus a sequence of wonderful examples of consistently high quality architecture.

This is true of the new Bartholomew County Jail, with its delightful scale and character. The design, full of the variety and articulation of so many of the town's older buildings carries forward, in a modern idiom, the mood of the courthouse with which it is so closely associated.

The domed outdoor recreation area over the elliptical inmate housing areas adds to the downtown a new visual landmark that can be seen, along with the "Campanile" of the courthouse from outside the town as it is approached. This combination of tower and dome, of courthouse and sheriff's detention center produces a wonderful metaphor of two associated functions and their related structures.

PROJECT
Bartholomew County Jail
Columbus, IN

CLIENT
Bartholomew County
Columbus, IN

ARCHITECTS
Hisaka & Associates
Berkeley, CA
in association with
Silver & Ziskind
New York, NY

PHOTOGRAPHER
Balthazar Korab
Troy, MI

FEDERAL CORRECTIONAL INSTITUTION

Sheridan, Oregon

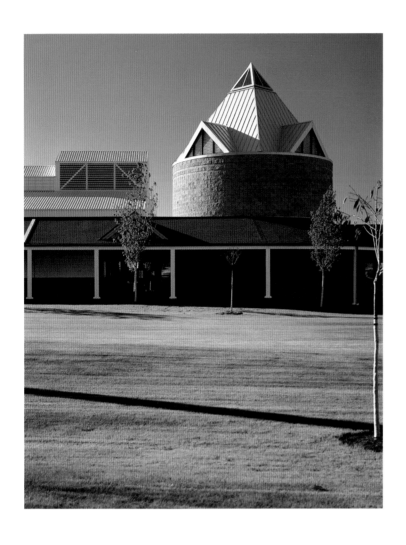

The Sheridan, Oregon, Bureau of Prison's facility displays a great variety of expression that is possible even within the limits of the prescribed space plans and general configuration of these correctional projects. Here, more than in many other examples, one sees a superb demonstration of how these basic building plans can be articulated and treated to produce a wholly residential scale modest in its exterior treatment for most of the facility, but peaked and capped with delightful formal accents of cupolas and roof top monitors.

The interior is an excellent example of carrying through the ideas of the varied and simply treated exteriors. The floor tile pattern gives scale to the otherwise uninterrupted floor plans and offers the user something closer to the residential quality of the exterior within the interior living spaces.

The treatment of spaces, varied as community areas and recreation halls, is consistent and unifies the many large open interior spaces. Whether the area be for quiet meditation or physically active sports, the spaces hold a sense of belonging with one another and show the undeniable fact that even within the constraints of a prototype design it is possible to obtain superb variants on the same theme from different creative designs.

PROJECT
Federal Correctional Institution
Sheridan, OR

CLIENT
U.S. Department of Justice
Federal Bureau of Prisons
Washington, DC

ARCHITECT
Zimmer Gunsul Frasca Partnership
Portland, OR

PHOTOGRAPHERS
Timothy Hursley
Little Rock, AR   (page 90, 92, 93 bottom)

Strode Eckert Photographic
Portland, OR   (all others)

BRISTOL COUNTY JAIL

North Dartmouth, Massachusetts

Low-rise county jails are more and more likely to become a model solution as smaller communities' expansion forces downtown facilities into the suburban areas around them. In many ways the low-rise facility produces an exceptional set of opportunities lacking at more compact sites in the center of our smaller cities.

Bristol County offers an excellent example of how such open sites and their low-rise facilities can produce a scale and character that is both humane and manageable. This facility is set in a low lying area off the main road. The feel is rural; the look normative. The simple materials of the construction are modulated with color changes and surface variations just enough to keep the scale at a level consistent with one-story buildings.

By "chaining" the buildings together to form both a security envelope and outside recreation areas, the look of the facility is quite residential and lacks the traditional symbols of a high security facility like towers and fences layered with row upon row of razor ribbon.

The modest scale of spaces created by linking the building complexes' individual structures and their treatment, make the mood of the facility serene and unintimidating.

PROJECT
Bristol County Jail
North Dartmouth, MA

CLIENT
Commonwealth of Massachusetts
Division of Capital Planning and Operations
Boston, MA

ARCHITECTS
Whitney Atwood Norcross Associates, Inc.
Boston, MA
in association with
Silver & Ziskind
New York, NY
and
Di Marinisi & Wolfe
Boston, MA

PHOTOGRAPHER
Douglas R. Gilbert
Newburyport, MA

LOOKOUT MOUNTAIN SCHOOL

Golden, Colorado

As a "jail" for juvenile offenders, Lookout Mountain represents a quality environment that recognizes the need for scale and a residential architectural character devoid of the traditional symbols of incarceration. The design of Lookout Mountain School demonstrates the qualities of being both less institutional and less intimidating than the traditional settings that are generally lacking any concern for the impact of the physical environment.

The campus setting, with its elegant entry areas and well-lit, spacious day areas, enhances the liveability of these facilities. The buildings are set in a turn-of-the-century campus and fit comfortably within this setting favored with pleasant views and access to the outdoors.

By mannering the architecture of these buildings to be less institutional, a less intimidating and friendlier campus has evolved which has had a positive influence on the lives and attitudes of juveniles who reside here.

PROJECT
Lookout Mountain School
Golden, CO

CLIENT
Colorado Division of Youth Services
Denver, CO

ARCHITECT
RNL Design
Denver, CO
Architect of record
Anderson Mason Dale P.C.
Denver, CO

PHOTOGRAPHER
Jerry Butts
Denver, CO

GOVERNMENT/ COMMUNITY FACILITIES

In the years before the turn of the last century, public structures were conceived of as a civic demonstration of the high values of our society. Every state government built its ornate capitol building eyeing the federal Capitol in Washington as its model.

Such a mentality dominated much of the public sector, and structures were erected that exemplified the commitment of a community to building civic facilities that expressed the power of government.

After World War I, the character of this environment changed. There was no longer a willingness to expend tax dollars on landmarks and government often retreated to the pragmatism of available commercial space devoid of character or the ability to inspire or give feeling of awe.

This pragmatism is surely one of the hallmarks of the American mind and shows itself as frequently in today's world with its high construction costs, as it did in the early part of this century.

It is, therefore, no small challenge for architects to develop designs that work as architecture, and not merely building, given the general lack of interest of the public and government agencies in expending any extra tax revenue in pursuit of design excellence.

Because of this fact it is of special importance when quality architecture is produced in these difficult design areas.

Projects that have the capacity to capture some of the grandeur of the past government structures, or have the humanistic scale and feeling we have so little of in our built environment, quickly call a good deal of attention to themselves. While the best of these efforts produce quality architecture, the result is all too often something that looks attractive but lacks the element of delight in its design.

The design of both governmental and community facilities needs a commitment to a higher standard of design and construction if the end result will lead to a world more visually delightful than our current community.

Therefore, the projects in this chapter are drawn from the most contemporary examples that demonstrate the ability of some architects to achieve a substantial level of design quality even when the available funding is limited.

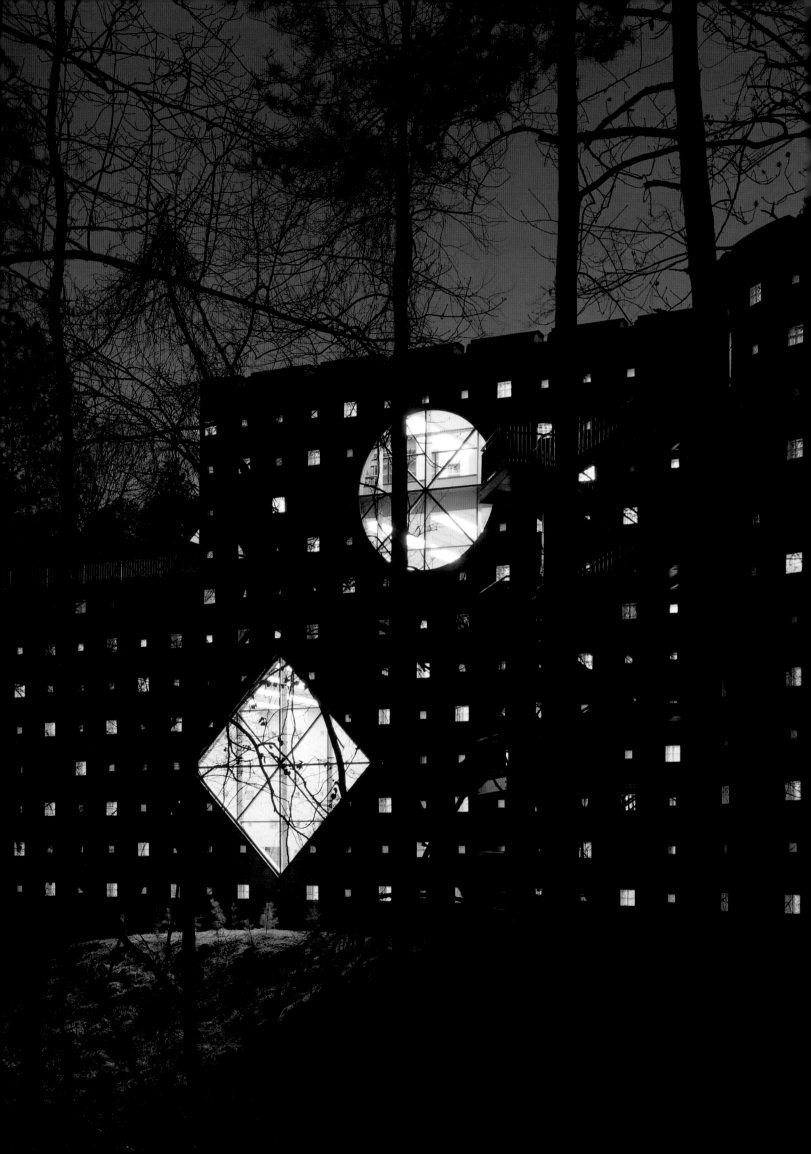

ADDITION TO TRINITY ELEMENTARY SCHOOL

Atlanta, Georgia

Everything about this project is instructive. It is formally and in detail, an especially successful example of design without the restraints of a fixed or limited vocabulary of modern minimalist rules. From its delightful colonnade to its cloister-like interiors, from its blue steel exterior stairway to its "night-wall" of glowing stars of light with its two "planetary" forms, the building is worth experiencing. The design is simply not restrained by conventional design wisdom, but full of small and delightful twists including twisted columns, "perforated" walls of glass block and an entry area built around a "pit" of stairs.

It is important to see this small project of only 250,000 square feet as a series of important design lessons about the potential of invention even in the most modest of programs.

What is also of interest is the fact that the building's materials are quite ordinary. It is rather the way in which they are used that is so special here; a way that is judicious and inventive.

Few buildings can sustain photographing them from every angle, but this structure reveals itself to have interest no matter how it is approached.

Its interior is no less successful in carrying out its mission of creating a truly special environment for those special human beings, our children.

PROJECT
Addition to Trinity Elementary School
Atlanta, GA

CLIENT
Trinity Elementary School
Atlanta, GA

ARCHITECT
Lord, Aeck & Sargent
Atlanta, GA

PHOTOGRAPHER
Jonathan Hillyer
Atlanta, GA

FULTON COUNTY GOVERNMENT CENTER

Atlanta, Georgia

Government complexes in the days after World War II were most often noted for their spartan simplicity, which when poorly executed epitomized boredom and banality. This is not an issue for the new Fulton County Government Center in Atlanta which in almost every aspect of its design makes a gesture toward variety, novelty and, at times, fanciful metaphor.

From the exterior curtain wall treatments, consisting of elements that reach perilously close to De-constructionist vocabularies, to the atrium interior dominated by a romantic Roman portico, the entire facility rings with excitement, that is ever changing as one moves about the building along the street or from within.

Even the choice of colors used in the chamber for the visitors seating stands out as another contrast to what has been experienced on the way to this space. There is something quite playful about all of this variety and contrast, yet it never appears to lose propriety in the process. While it lacks the somber tradition of bygone days, it does possess a civic quality appearing to state that this community likes life, enjoys its visual pleasures and rates things beyond their merely utilitarian value.

It is a structure in contrast to this older-part-of-town's historical paradigms that could have been used as a basis for the design. This states the significance of looking back to sober precedents and toward the future for excitement, variety, and new experiences.

PROJECT
Fulton County Government Center
Atlanta, GA

CLIENT
Fulton County Building Authority
Atlanta, GA

ARCHITECT
Rosser International, Inc.
Atlanta, GA
in joint venture with
Turner Associates
Atlanta, GA

PHOTOGRAPHER
Jeffrey Jacobs
Memphis, TN

ADDITION TO ATLANTA CITY HALL

Atlanta, Georgia

A more traditional approach to a government center than the nearby Fulton County Government Center, the Atlanta City Hall is a strictly modern building with forms and details barely covered with slight and delicate ornamentation. The large atrium with layered balconies and classic ornamental stairs makes a traditional statement about government and the relationship to the citizenry who use it. This is a facility whose design continues the long-established history of government displaying its power and in some respect creating a sense of civic pride by a combination of awe and monumental scale.

The sober colors of the chamber, reinforced by the extensive use of wood paneling, is a continuation and reinforcement of the essential theme of governmental power and authority. What is so successful in the design is the consistency of expression. Once having defined the aesthetic of dignity that would describe the environment, the execution of the design is superbly loyal to its original conceptual goal.

PROJECT
Addition to Atlanta City Hall
Atlanta, GA

CLIENT
City of Atlanta, GA
Atlanta, GA

ARCHITECT
Jova/Daniels/Busby
Atlanta, GA

PHOTOGRAPHER
James S. Roof
Duluth, GA

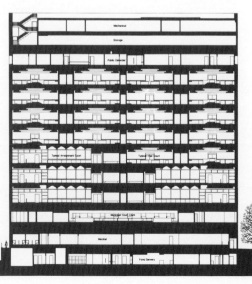

VAN NUYS COURTS BUILDING

Van Nuys, California

Glass, by its very nature, creates a dual world of the one reflected off its surface and the world enclosed behind it. It is for this reason that the use of glass over large expanses presents special formal problems. Left to its own devices it can result in confusing and perhaps surrealist effects, but if controlled, can produce a predictable sense of these two worlds of inside and outside almost simultaneously.

The Van Nuys Municipal Courts building is a particularly interesting example of a glass block enclosed or encircled by a solid frame of building delimiting its boundaries and strongly focusing the eye on the central entry element. The glass cylinder set beneath the main glass wall is the central visual feature of this highly symmetrical geometric form. Its circular theme is repeated throughout the building.

As with so many urban structures it is forced to the limits of its site defined by the street pattern and thereby made to stand alone. But, despite this civic landscape limitation, the building truly rises above its mundane setting to be a successful expression of high quality civic design in the best sense of modern architecture.

PROJECT
Van Nuys Courts Building
Van Nuys, CA

CLIENT
County of Los Angeles
Los Angeles, CA

ARCHITECT
Dworsky Associates, Inc.
Los Angeles, CA

PHOTOGRAPHER
Tom Bonner
Venice, CA

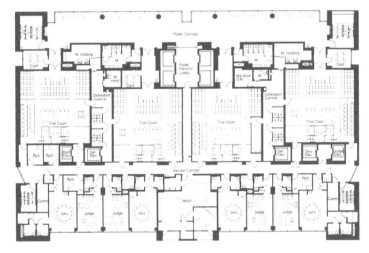

NO TALKING WHILE COURT IS IN SESSION

LOVELAND CIVIC CENTER AND MUNICIPAL BUILDING

Loveland, Colorado

It is typical to expect large city and county centers and their court houses to be monumental and impressive, but it is in the case of smaller communities that striving for such scale results in pretentious and threatening architecture. It is far more difficult to design sensitively scaled government structures when they are modest in size.

The Loveland Municipal Complex is a carefully conceived combination of modest structures of a restrained design which derives its impact and character from its setting along a body of water, and the way it is grouped on a corner site. The buildings themselves have no distinctive details, but represent how a careful use of traditional forms and details can produce a building complex which has the scale and character appropriate to smaller community projects. Even the blue glass bridge between the two structures, one an old school house adapted to its new use and the other a new structure, is so low key that it tends to recede from view despite its prominent location.

The siting of the entry and the walk under the glass bridge to the display beyond, are the kinds of understated design features appropriate to a small city not seeking to garishly imitate large urban communities.

PROJECT
Loveland Civic Center and Municipal Building
Loveland, CO

CLIENT
City of Loveland
Loveland, CO

ARCHITECT
Midyette-Seieroe-Hartronft
Boulder, CO

PHOTOGRAPHER
Robert W. Springate

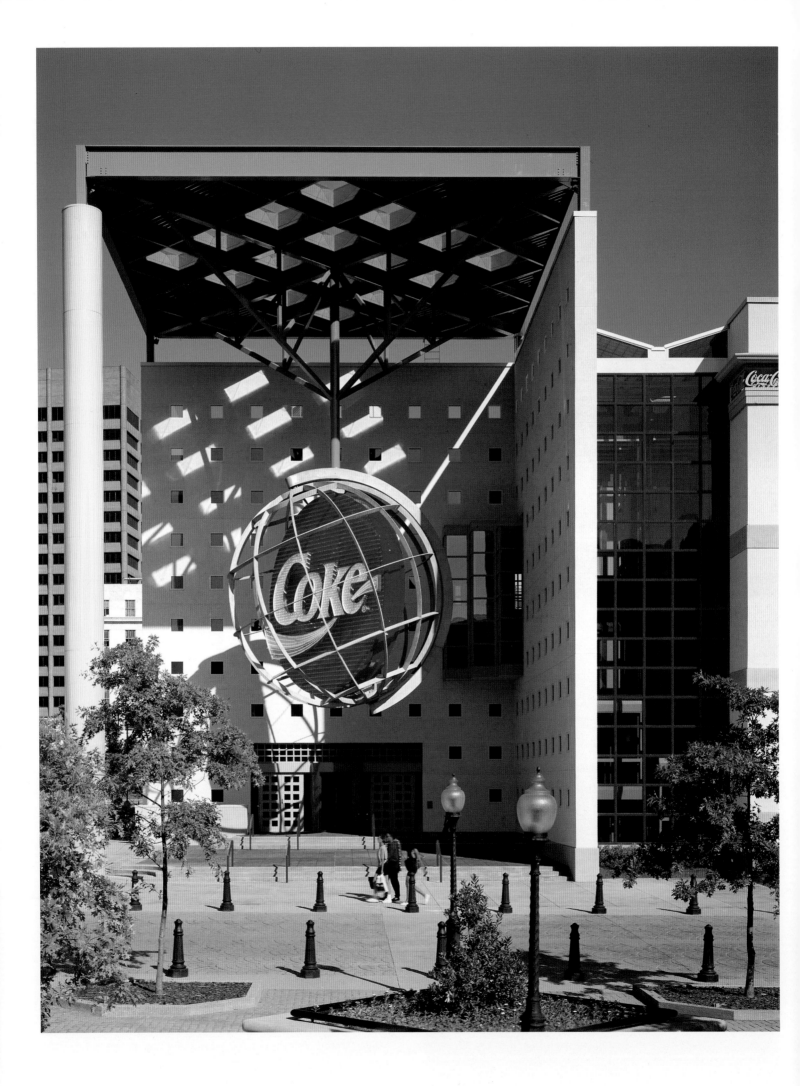

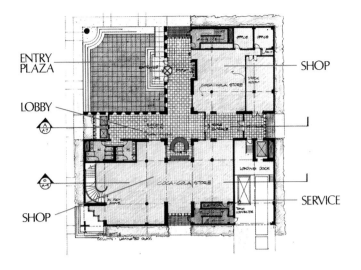

ENTRY PLAZA — SHOP

LOBBY

SHOP — SERVICE

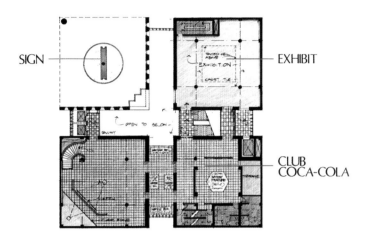

SIGN — EXHIBIT

CLUB COCA-COLA

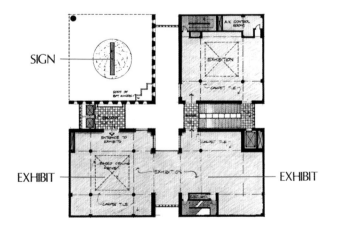

SIGN

EXHIBIT — EXHIBIT

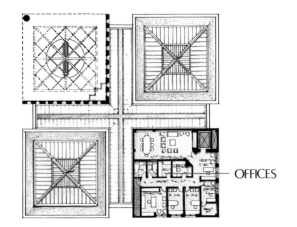

OFFICES

THE WORLD OF COCA-COLA PAVILION
Atlanta, Georgia

When a large public corporation like Coca-Cola decides to build a public use building intended to exhibit itself at its best, it raises issues about the message, the medium and how it fits into its context. It is a credit to Coca-Cola that their Pavilion is a playful project, done with the kind of fancifulness that makes it what it should be, a fun place to see and visit.

This is clearly no somber effort to convey corporate power, but rather a place full of color and light and changing experiences that lead a viewer around a miniature "museum."

Even the forms that comprise the four interconnected pavilions are treated differently from one another to give even greater variety and playfulness to this grouping of building blocks.

The exhibition pavilion is set within a park with a fountain at the focus of the plaza facing the entry to the building. Because of its location and siting on structure it clearly distinguishes itself from the surrounding setting. It is in fact the center of its own context and creates a new setting in contrast to that along the horizon.

The interior is in the best tradition of exhibition pavilions and convention centers, replete with visual variety and built for ease of circulation.

PROJECT
The World of Coca-Cola Pavilion
Atlanta, GA

CLIENT
The Coca-Cola Company
Atlanta, GA

ARCHITECT
Thompson, Ventulett, Stainback & Associates, Inc.
Atlanta, GA
Associate Architect, Design Consultant
Turner Associates/Architects & Planners, Inc.
Atlanta, GA

PHOTOGRAPHER
Timothy Hursley
Little Rock, AR

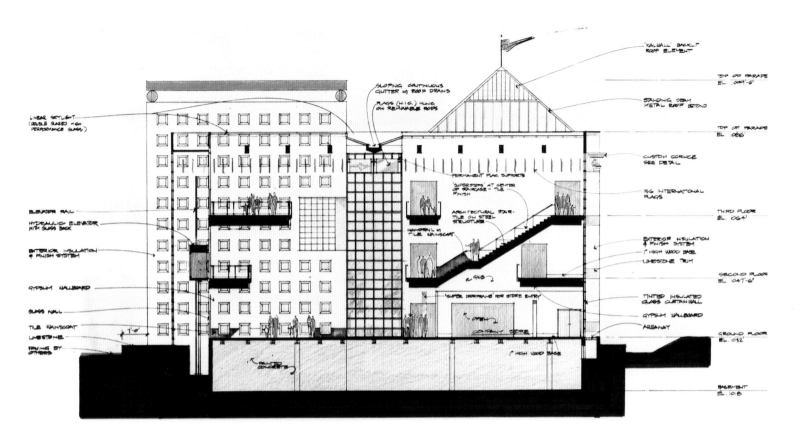

KALWALL BACKLIT
ROOF ELEMENT

TOP OF PARAPET
EL. 089'-6"

SLOPING CONTINUOUS
GUTTER W/ ROOF DRAINS

STANDING SEAM
METAL ROOF BEYOND

FLAGS (H.I.C.) HUNG
ON REMOVABLE RODS

LINEAR SKYLIGHT
(DOUBLE GLAZED HIGH
PERFORMANCE GLASS)

TOP OF PARAPET
EL. 086'

CUSTOM CORNICE
SEE DETAIL

PERMANENT FLAG SUPPORTS

156 INTERNATIONAL
FLAGS

SUPERSTEPS AT CENTER
OF STAIRCASE - TILE
FINISH

THIRD FLOOR
EL. 064'

ELEVATOR RAIL

ARCHITECTURAL STAIR-
TILE ON STEEL
STRUCTURE

HYDRAULIC ELEVATOR
WITH GLASS BACK

EXTERIOR INSULATION
& FINISH SYSTEM

EXTERIOR INSULATION
& FINISH SYSTEM

HANDRAIL IN
TILE WAINSCOT

1" HIGH WOOD BASE

LIMESTONE TRIM

R 9N3

GYPSUM WALLBOARD

SECOND FLOOR
EL. 047'-6"

GLASS WALL

'SUPER DOORFRAME' FOR STORE ENTRY

TINTED INSULATED
GLASS CURTAIN WALL

OPEN

GYPSUM WALLBOARD

TILE WAINSCOT

COMPANY STORE

AREAWAY

LIMESTONE

GROUND FLOOR
EL. 032'

PAVING BY
OTHERS

PAINTED
CONCRETE

1" HIGH WOOD BASE

BASEMENT
EL. 1018'

PHOENIX CITY HALL

Phoenix, Arizona

Street patterns have for ages dominated the character of cities. They often arbitrarily divide areas so that it becomes necessary for designers to create ways of uniting what are in fact, unified spaces fragmented by streets. The Phoenix City Hall has had to deal with an existing street pattern, that if followed religiously, would have provided no space for the public outside the walls of the building itself. Even at its best, only a small portion of the building's site could be dedicated to a public outdoor space, so it became necessary to find a means of linking one site, the City Hall site, with an adjacent park setting across the street. By curving the building's facade back from the street the building forms an entry facade or arcade leading to a glass vaulted atrium. Through the use of paving patterns and a "line" leading from the building's street entrance to the park across the street, the facility and park are successfully linked. The building derives its form from the shape of the site and the way the entry plaza is generated.

The building's exterior combines a strictly modern articulation with a postmodern layering of forms onto, and through one another. In this sense, it is an interesting combination of influences which places a relatively small emphasis on massing while mainly concerning itself with surfaces and their treatments. There is something implied in the detail that recalls early twentieth-century neo-Gothic office towers like the Woolworth building in New York, without its full-fledged tower.

The building's relation to its site and the use of paving patterns and a line leading from the building's street entrance to the park help it cross the artificial barrier of sidewalks and a roadway.
*Construction Completed January, 1994

PROJECT
Phoenix City Hall
Phoenix, AZ

CLIENT
City of Phoenix
Phoenix, AZ

ARCHITECT
Langdon Wilson Architecture Planning
Phoenix, AZ

PHOTOGRAPHER
Mark Lohman
Los Angeles, CA

SAN JOAQUIN COUNTY HUMAN SERVICES AGENCY BUILDING

Stockton, California

San Joaquin County Human Services Agency Building, with its tunnel vaulted atrium of glass and lacy steel framing, covers a substantial part of an entire urban block. While only an average of three stories, the sheer ground coverage makes the complex appear quite large. The architect has attempted to control the sense of size. This is achieved with a combination of articulating surfaces and by subdividing the facade along its length into rectangular and curved sub-units. By cutting and shaping the corners, the design of the two adjacent facades is made to vary from a common theme, enough to give each street wall its own distinctive treatment, while preserving the essential character. The entry facade recalls the scale of more traditional masonry load bearing buildings of the past, and through the device of a strongly articulated entry archway, creates a strong contrast between delicate transparency, a vaulted skylight and the solidity of stone and brick.

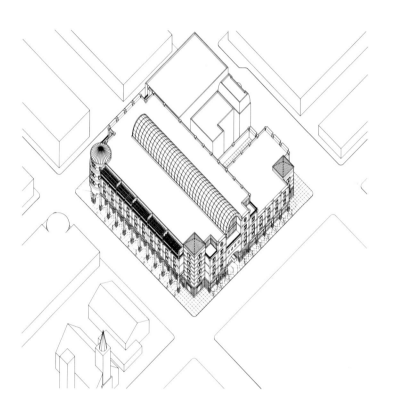

PROJECT
San Joaquin County Human Services Agency Building
Stockton, CA

CLIENT
County of San Joaquin
Stockton, CA

ARCHITECT
Albert C. Martin & Associates
Los Angeles, CA

PHOTOGRAPHERS
David Hewitt/Anne Garrison
San Diego, CA

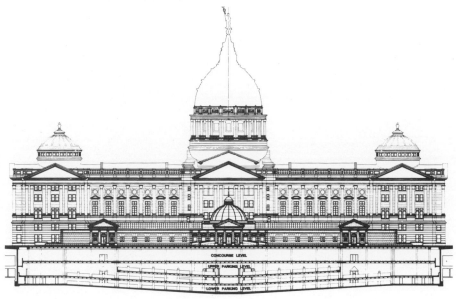

EAST WING ADDITION TO PENNSYLVANIA STATE CAPITOL CAPITOL COMPLEX

Harrisburg, Pennsylvania

If high drama can be attributed to an architectural design then capital cities with their government centers are probably the most notable examples of such places. One sees it in the Vatican in Rome, and in Paris and London.

The United States has surely one of the world's most notable examples in Washington, DC, but it is almost as rare as eagles to find truly successful examples among the 50 state capitols in this country.

Pennsylvania is an exception though, where the recently renovated capitol complex is an extraordinarily successful example of such high drama. It is sheer virtuosity in an eclectic style. In many ways it demonstrates a quality of historical styles lost to those who grew up imbued by modernism, and, by training, hostile to all classical styles. What is so special about this is its sheer beauty and elegance of its shadowed surface sweeping form which cover, what appears to be acres of civic ground.

It is a significant example of why completing original concepts as they were conceived is often more likely to produce a successful effect rather than slavishly forcing a current stylistic model onto an older order.

PROJECT
East Wing Addition to Pennsylvania State Capitol
Capitol Complex
Harrisburg, PA

CLIENT
Department of General Services
Harrisburg, PA

ARCHITECT
Celli-Flynn and Associates
Pittsburgh, PA

PHOTOGRAPHER
Thorney Lieberman
Boulder, CO

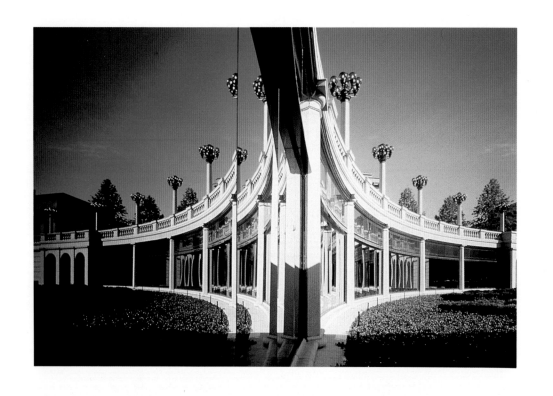

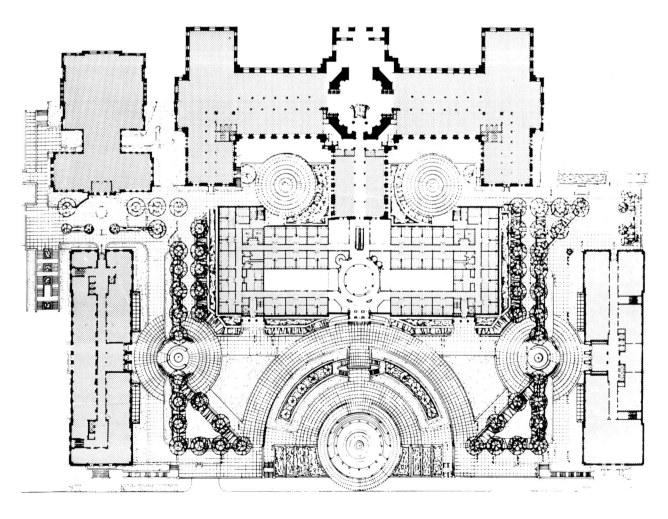

THE WILLIAM C. WARDLAW JR. CENTER GEORGIA INSTITUTE OF TECHNOLOGY

Atlanta, Georgia

The William C. Wardlaw Jr. Center is a multi-purpose building used by various departments and foundations at the Georgia Tech Campus in Atlanta. It is literally a replacement structure inserted in the place of demolished perimeter stands that once enclosed the south side of the school's football stadium.

It derives its form from its role as a replacement structure. It is always interesting to see how architecture can develop in context of an odd or contrived nature. This site and its shape are as arbitrary a set of site conditions as one could imagine. It is, therefore, quite a pleasant surprise to see a structure that works aesthetically even when forced into an unconventional mold. To exploit the formal consequences of such odd sites it is often necessary to exaggerate one dimension of the building. In small urban sites in the downtown business areas of our cities, the solution is most often a strong vertical emphasis. In low-rise situations, as is the case of this center, a strong horizontal pattern acts to unify the curved facade while avoiding a sense of endless repetition horizontally. On the whole, the materials of concrete and stone are simpler in their design and composition than they appear, but by the judicious cutting out of window openings, what would become an unrelentless set of horizontal bands, instead, becomes wonderfully articulated and varied. The pattern set-up by the stone bandings and the windows set within them, makes the entry wall sufficiently fluid in its ability to take varied surface treatment within much of any modification in the basic building masses.

PROJECT
The William C. Wardlaw Jr. Center
Georgia Institute of Technology
Atlanta, GA

CLIENT
Georgia Tech Foundation
Atlanta, GA

ARCHITECT
Jova/Daniels/Busby
Atlanta, GA

PHOTOGRAPHER
James S. Roof
Duluth, GA

UNITED STATES EMBASSY COMPLEX

San Salvador, El Salvador

Over the last four administrations in Washington, DC, the government has attempted to upgrade, renew and substantially replace American embassies around the world. Many of these buildings have sought to capture the feelings of the native architecture. All too often the result is kitschy, bad imitation.

In El Salvador, the U.S. Embassy clearly reflects a Latin American approach to the way buildings are shaped and how they are treated and completed both inside and out.

Designed as a small village-like community, the embassy compound is tied together as a series of separated structures by the fact of a simple set of design elements including a monochromatic facade and a clearly "standardized" pattern of window openings. There is a feeling about the setting that it is a pedestrian's world and that one could feel comfortable walking about the facility. Because the building's elements are randomly scattered throughout the site, the result is an open view campus with sheltered walkways alongside buildings leading to open spaces lacking any negative sense of confinement.

There are portions of the interior that effectively carry out the qualities of mass and solidity observed on the facades of the various buildings of the compound.

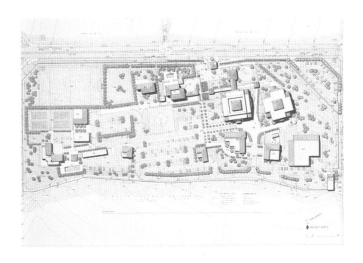

PROJECT
United States Embassy Complex
San Salvador, El Salvador

CLIENT
United States Department of State
Office of Foreign Building Operations
Washington, DC

ARCHITECT
CRSS Architects, Inc.
Houston, TX

PHOTOGRAPHER
Greg Hursley
Austin, TX

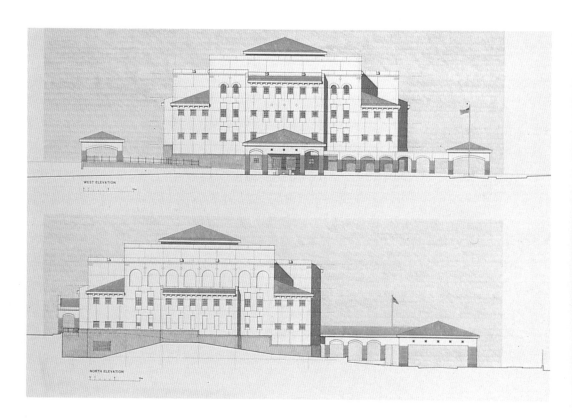

WEST ELEVATION

NORTH ELEVATION

BOULDER
PUBLIC LIBRARY

Boulder, Colorado

There appears to be hardly a place in Colorado where the view of the mountain peaks and surrounding hillsides is not spectacular; it definitely calls for our buildings to exploit the drama themselves.

The Boulder Public Library is a mountain range of forms, all of which link together in a varied and interesting way. The materials of glass and concrete represent a simple vocabulary in contrast to the complex and variegated forms of the building. The circular stairway supports the overall concept of transparency and layered spaces visible through several sheets of glass. There is no attempt to use color to reinforce these strong forms because they stand upon their shapes and scale so well. Whether in the interior or reviewing the exterior, the details give way to the power of the forms and their considerable amount of transparency.

PROJECT
Boulder Public Library
Boulder, CO

CLIENT
City of Boulder
Boulder, CO

ARCHITECT
Midyette-Seieroe-Hartronft
Boulder, CO
Design Architect:
Eugene Aubrey, FAIA
Anna Maria, FL

PHOTOGRAPHER
©1992 Andrew Kramer, AIA
Boulder, CO

ERIE COMMUNITY COLLEGE ATHLETIC CENTER

Buffalo, New York

Context in urban settings has always been viewed as an essential aspect of design. The new must somehow be at ease with the old and must not strive to be more than its appropriate role would indicate. Being opposite, the extraordinary neo-Gothic old Buffalo Post Office is a challenging location since the building is both powerful in detail and substantial in size. This building covers an entire city block, so setting a new structure opposite of equal size raises all sorts of questions of scale, proportion, detail and, above all else, the role of context.

The new Athletic Center for the Erie Community College takes a rather unique approach by configuring each facade of the building in a manner which in significant ways makes it contextual to its street wall facade or adjacent structure across the street. The facade opposite the old post office is clearly full of Gothic recall, the entry walk which is parallel to the street reminds one of a public gathering space, while the side one sees when merely turning the corner, possesses the form and rhythm expected in a classic railroad station or other large spaced public building. The other two facades are dramatic contrasts of glass and panel walls quite contemporary by contrast and linked together expertly so as never to feel alien to one another.

* All photographs shown here are construction photographs, as the project was still being completed when the Center was photographed.

PROJECT
Erie Community College Athletic Center
Buffalo, NY

CLIENT
Erie Community College & The Erie County
Department of Environment & Planning
Buffalo, NY
Dormitory Authority, State of New York
Albany, NY

ARCHITECT
Hamilton Houston Lownie Architects, PC
Buffalo, NY

PHOTOGRAPHER
Biff Henrich
Buffalo, NY

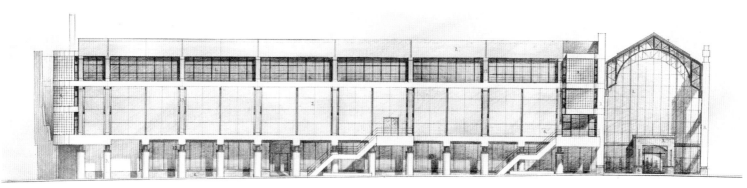

South Division / North

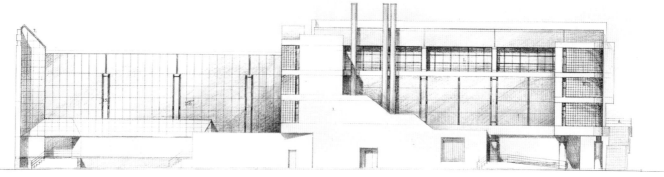

Elm Street / East

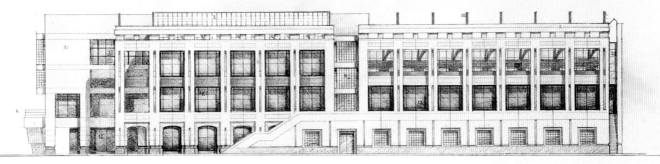

Oak Street / West

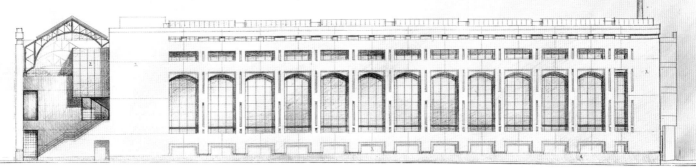

Swan Street / South

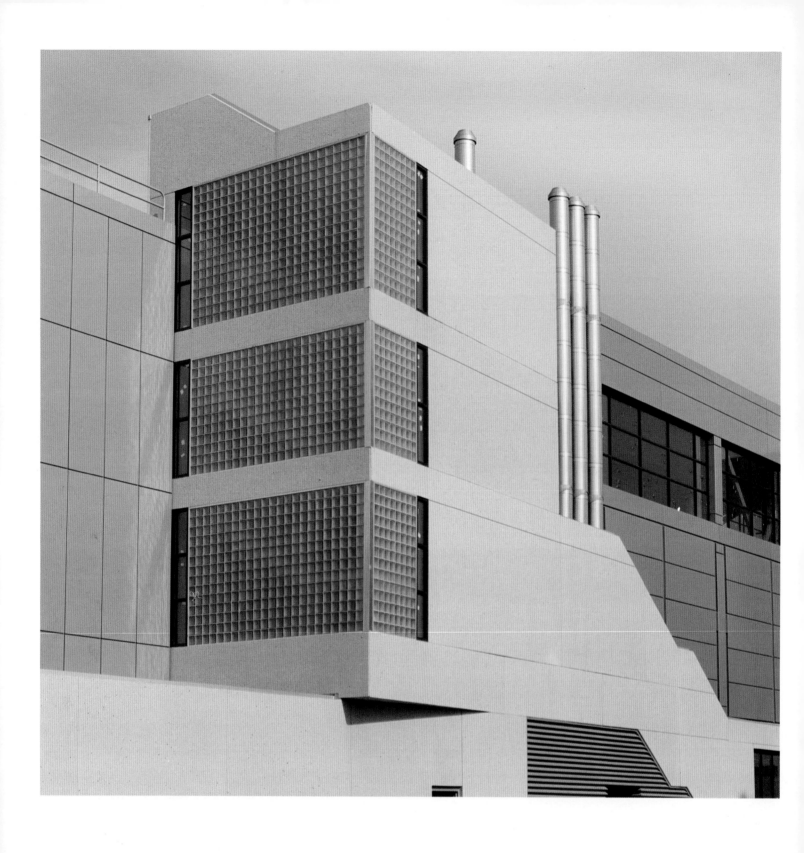

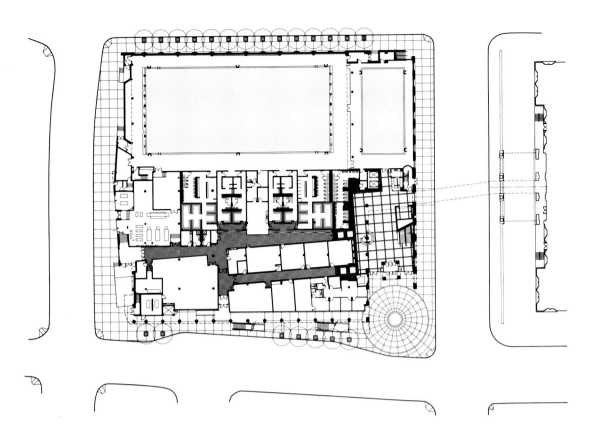

THE PIERPONT MORGAN LIBRARY

New York, New York

Adding onto a universally admired landmark, even when the addition is modest in scale and size, is fraught with the potential of disastrous damage to an important civic possession. The Pierpont Morgan Library is such a civic possession in the congested environs of New York City.

The addition of an enclosed space to be used as a garden court required an exceptional degree of care to make the new construction relate and compliment the existing structure. The choice of what is essentially a greenhouse form of metal and glass, in combination with graceful curved steel arches forms a highly singular visual statement, which is quite special in itself. It is surprisingly modest and has no negative effect on the existing building, and seems to be perfectly natural and at home with its newer neighbor.

The interior is restrained in the same manner as the exterior, contributing to a harmonious whole. The curves of the roof are recalled in the curved face of the balcony and its sweeping brass and white metal handrails. One particularly pleasant feature of the design is the subdued colors of stone and metalwork. Except for the brass handrails, the space has a singular unity of color that could easily be boring. However, the variety of texture and tone found in the floors and walls provide relief from this possibility.

PROJECT
The Pierpont Morgan Library
New York, NY

CLIENT
The Pierpont Morgan Library
New York, NY

ARCHITECT
Voorsanger & Associates, Architects, P.C.
New York, NY

PHOTOGRAPHER
Paul Warchol
New York, NY

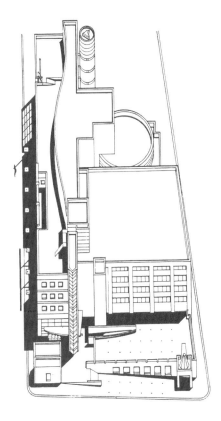

EUGENIO MARIA DE HOSTOS COMMUNITY COLLEGE ALLIED HEALTH CENTER

Bronx, New York

The Modern movement was officially declared dead in the mid-eighties by all those who saw in the style the signs of aesthetic exhaustion that defines the end of an artistic period. The only thing that they neglected to notice was that it was far from exhausted, merely awaiting the phase of refinement and subtle evolution that revitalized an aging movement.

Hostos Community College in New York is among the best of its genre, elegant and alive with visual excitement and spaces so varied, yet so well bound together as to be a vivid demonstration of how much variety one can achieve in an environment designed around the minimalist rules of the Modern movement.

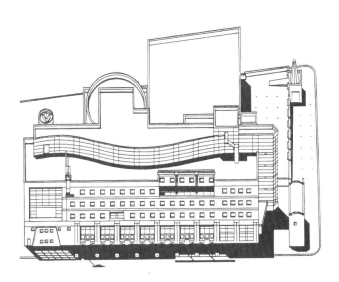

From the reading room with its light-cylinders to the "porch" with its floating balconies, the detail is so elegantly refined and tastefully restrained that, in isolation it appears almost ordinary, but together the effect produces wonderful spaces with a much greater sense of variety than implied by any individual design element.

Even the colorful day care center, with its strong geometric forms seems perfectly consistent with the far more subdued hues of the balance of the building. In so many aspects of this project one sees the vindication of the best of a set of stylistic principles that have unfairly been condemned as no longer valid. It is encouraging to see that diversity in style can occur even in a society where a belief in the "truth" on one style at a time has dominated the creative process in the arts for ages.

PROJECT
Eugenio Maria de Hostos Community College
Allied Health Center
Bronx, NY

CLIENT
The City University of New York
New York, NY
Dormitory Authority of the State of New York
Albany, NY

ARCHITECT
Voorsanger & Associates, Architects, P.C.
New York, NY
in association with
Hirsch Danois Architects, P.C.
New York, NY

PHOTOGRAPHER
Paul Warchol
New York, NY

OREGON CONVENTION CENTER
Portland, Oregon

Convention Centers are hardly the building type treated with aesthetic indifference as is the history of so many other American building types. But it has consistently suffered from a preoccupation with a strong singular visual statement at the expense of almost everything else. As a result of this tendency these enormous and repetitive designs quickly grow boring and lose any long-term ability to provide anything more than a functional setting.

What makes the Oregon Convention Center worth special attention is that, while it possesses a strong overall, if not singular feeling, it does not do so at the expense of visual variety and spatial diversity. In fact, the building appears quite different from different perspectives, bound together only by the two pylons of glass that became its landmark feature along the skyline.

The interior design is also quite different from the singular spaces that characterize so many of the recently built convention centers. It is more like the setting we associate with elegant hotels and other corporate style settings where there is a clear message that conveys the notion that the user is in a place away from the ordinary and full of unpredictable discoveries which are hidden in the corners and around the bend of every corridor.

PROJECT
Oregon Convention Center
Portland, OR

CLIENT
Metropolitan Service District
Portland, OR

ARCHITECT
Zimmer Gunsul Frasca Partnership
Portland, OR

PHOTOGRAPHER
Timothy Hursley
Little Rock, AR (all others)

Strode Eckert Photographic
Portland, OR (page 178 bottom)

GLENCASTLE

Atlanta, Georgia

Some of the greatest challenges for designers come from situations involving transforming a structure from one limiting use to another equally limiting one. GlenCastle, a shutter prison in Atlanta, was converted into low-income housing. It is not merely the disparity of uses, but the fact that their physical demands are so in opposition to one another that makes this kind of transposition so difficult. To do it well, often requires considerable funding, so it is worth noting when such a transposition is successfully completed with labor and materials donated by the professionals involved with the project.

To quote the architect who has stated it quite well, "This 104-year-old debtors prison was transformed into 67 low-income housing units. Built in 1887, this magnificent building with twin turrets and 42-inch thick walls stood empty for years before being transformed into a never before seen public housing development in Atlanta. Former rooms of oppression were turned into rooms of hope. The prison blacksmith shop was renovated into a chapel and day care center. The project was completed solely by time, labor and material donated by numerous contractors throughout Atlanta."

The goal of maintaining the historic integrity of the building exterior has clearly been met. This is consistent with the goal of transforming the interior into an environment that meets contemporary standards for family living.

It is not without reason that the scale and character of the exterior was preserved. The building's form represents both its past and uses and its future potential as an adaptive reuse.

PROJECT
GlenCastle
Atlanta, GA

CLIENT
Family Consulting Services
Charis Housing
Atlanta, GA

ARCHITECT
Bradfield, Richards & Associates, Architects, Inc.
Atlanta, GA

PHOTOGRAPHER
Jean and John Williams
Marietta, GA

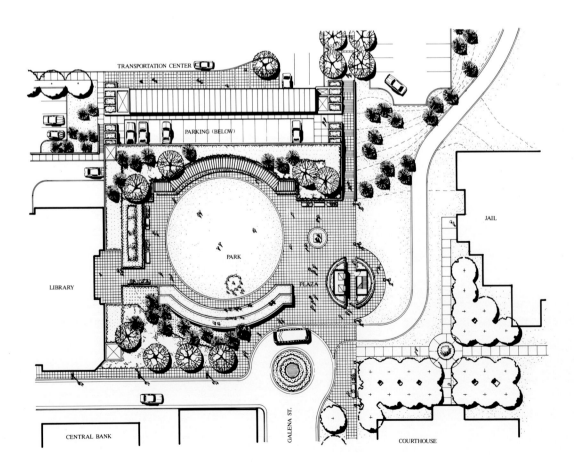

RIO GRANDE PARKING FACILITY AND TRANSPORTATION CENTER

Aspen, Colorado

Urban spaces are so often what is left over from the pattern of streets defined by surveyors and not covered with the products of speculators and developers. The leftover "civic" space is often treated as if it were a nuisance to be paved over and made available for parking and waiting taxis.

When a small urban space like that in Aspen, Colorado, was developed into a truly public environment which gave the city a new civic space, the effort, both to create and finally find and build it needed to be properly appreciated.

The scale of this delightful park united with a commuter/tourist transportation center and set over an underground garage on a gently sloping hill, is modest, familiar and above all else human. There is no forced monument here, merely a pleasant public space with pleasing detailed small structures consistently designed, but with varying functions.

The Rio Grande project demonstrates how it is possible to achieve a successful urban space with the demand of traffic and pedestrian movement without ending up with a dull and dehumanizing parking and transportation center dominating a central public area.

PROJECT
Rio Grande Parking Facility and Transportation Center
Aspen, CO

CLIENT
City of Aspen
Aspen, CO

ARCHITECT
RNL Design
Denver, CO
Associate Architect
Gibson & Reno Architects
Aspen, CO

PHOTOGRAPHER
Jerry Butts
Denver, CO

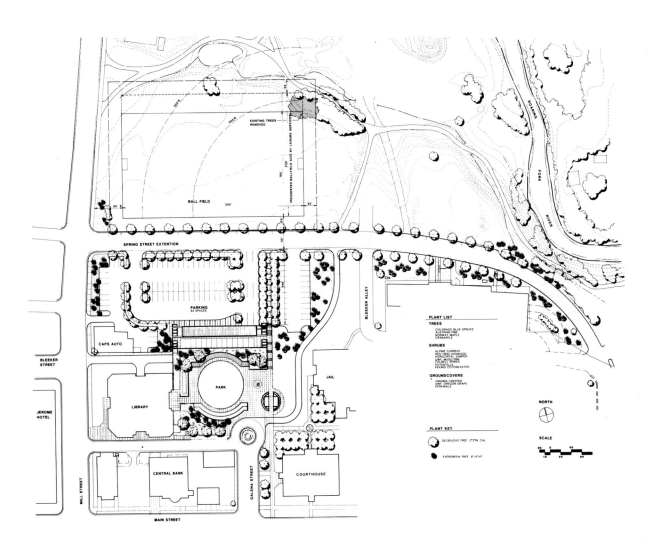

PLANT LIST

TREES
COLORADO BLUE SPRUCE
AUSTRIAN PINE
NORWAY MAPLE
CRABAPPLE

SHRUBS
ALPINE CURRENT
RED-TWIG DOGWOOD
HORIZONTAL JUNIPER
DWF. MUGO PINE
FOLBELL SPIREA
POTENTILLA
PEKING COTONEASTER

GROUNDCOVERS
VIRGINIA CREEPER
DWF. OREGON GRAPE
PERENNIALS

NORTH

PLANT KEY

DECIDUOUS TREE 2"3" IN. CAL.

EVERGREEN TREE 8'-10' HT.

SCALE

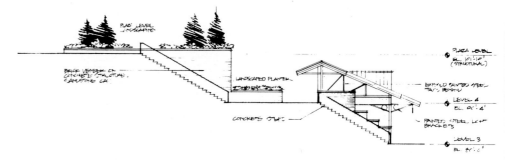

EAST ELEVATION
SCALE 1/8"=1'-0"

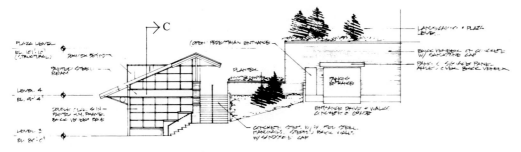

WEST ELEVATION
SCALE 1/8"=1'-0"

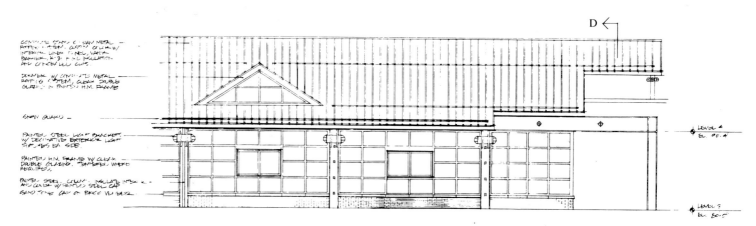

PARTIAL NORTH ELEVATION
SCALE 1/4"=1'-0"

FULLER E. CALLAWAY, JR., MANUFACTURING RESEARCH CENTER GEORGIA INSTITUTE OF TECHNOLOGY

Atlanta, Georgia

Modern architects have typically had difficulties with design metaphors. Possibly because we are a society without the myths and legends of our classical ancestors, we have no stories to tell or tales to recall about ourselves to justify or make comprehensible metaphors. Probably the closest thing we have to a cultural mythology is our faith and respect in the capacity of technology to create a better world or to solve the current epidemic. So, it seems appropriate to see the use of metaphor in the design of a structure associated with technology and clearly intended to be an environment loaded with such technological similes. Whether it is the warm geared columns at the entry or the "gear" dropped ceiling in the lecture center, the design of the Fuller E. Callaway Manufacturing Research Center uses this simple element to act as both ornament and metaphor of technology and research. What is pleasing about its use is in the employed restraint; it is not overdone and slavishly repeated at every opportunity. The message is made at strategic locations and the rest of the building is left to express its function directly without the need of ornamentation or metaphorical adornment.

The interior reinforces the "industrial" look of the exterior with its bold forms and color. There is no false modesty here. The eye is filled with color and texture of many sorts but the unity of line and color are so strong that even the diversity of detail seems perfectly correct.

PROJECT
Fuller E. Callaway, Jr., Manufacturing Research Center
Georgia Institute of Technology
Atlanta, GA

CLIENT
Georgia Institute of Technology
Atlanta, GA

ARCHITECT
Lord, Aeck & Sargent
Atlanta, GA

PHOTOGRAPHER
Jonathan Hillyer
Atlanta, GA

CAMP TWEEDALE WINTERIZED CABIN COMPLEX AND ACTIVITY BUILDING

Chester County, Pennsylvania

While Camp Tweedale is full of historical recall it is hardly stuck in mere imitation. On the contrary it is executed with an exceptional degree of conviction to a high quality of spatial design and detail. The natural setting is never compromised and the individual structures are designed around a simple consistent vocabulary of details, forms, colors and materials. The strong roof lines and harmonious color of the shingles and building walls gives these earth tone structures a strong sense of being part of their setting in a very organic way.

The interiors carry the exterior quality right through every corner of the buildings and create the feeling of being one with the setting an essential part of the experience of this project. Camp Tweedale is no mere "woodsy" looking project; it is a serious application of important design principles about how architecture fits into its natural setting and how space is created without destroying the fabric of a natural setting. The structures are carefully situated, so as not to be packed close together; this makes moving about a continuous "nature" experience and places the user into the role of active participant instead of casual observer.

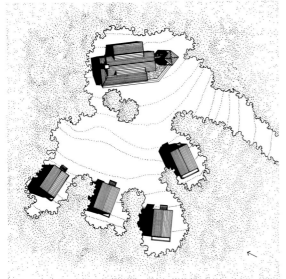

PROJECT
Camp Tweedale
Winterized Cabin Complex and Activity Building
Chester County, PA

CLIENT
Freedom Valley Girl Scout Council
Valley Forge, PA

ARCHITECT
Susan Maxman Architects
Philadelphia, PA

PHOTOGRAPHERS
Tom Bernard
Berwyn, PA   (all others)

Susan A. Maxman, FAIA
Philadelphia, PA   (all drawings)

Jeffrey C. Hayes, AIA
Philadelphia, PA   (page 195 top)

Second Floor

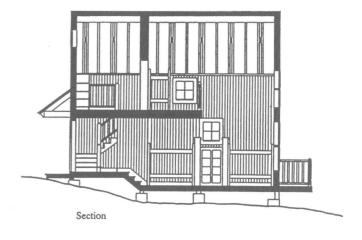

Section

First Floor

0   10

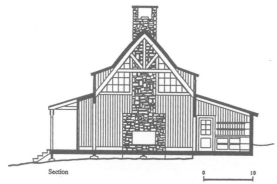

Section

0   10

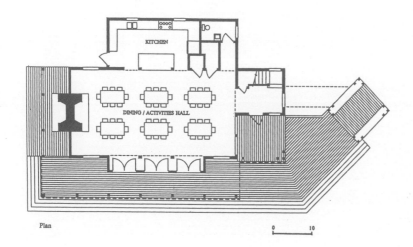

Plan

0   10

THE LIVING WORLD AT THE ST. LOUIS ZOO

St. Louis, Missouri

All too often the environment associated with housing animals or animal-related exhibits places all of its emphasis on the functional aspects of the building design problem without ever concerning itself with the opportunity to produce a setting which makes the experience both delightful and entertaining.

The Living World at the St. Louis Zoo produces an environment that is comfortable and pleasing to the eye, enhancing the experience of moving through the facility. The central space is domed with a translucent structure, that makes arrival at the building pleasant and the first of a series of interconnecting spaces including a media-rich exhibit hall full of large screens and a giant squid.

The character is so simple and so pleasing, that the spaces lend an aura of domestic scale and a comfortable feeling of a place where one could have lots of fun. In this environment, designed to show animal diversity, ecology and conservation, every effort appears dedicated to showing how easy it is to achieve a combination of family entertainment and education.

PROJECT
The Living World at the St. Louis Zoo
St. Louis, MO

CLIENT
St. Louis Zoo
St. Louis, MO

ARCHITECT
Hellmuth, Obata & Kassabaum, Inc.
St. Louis, MO

PHOTOGRAPHERS
Bob Pettus
St. Louis, MO   (page 203 bottom)

George Cott
Tampa, FL   (all others)

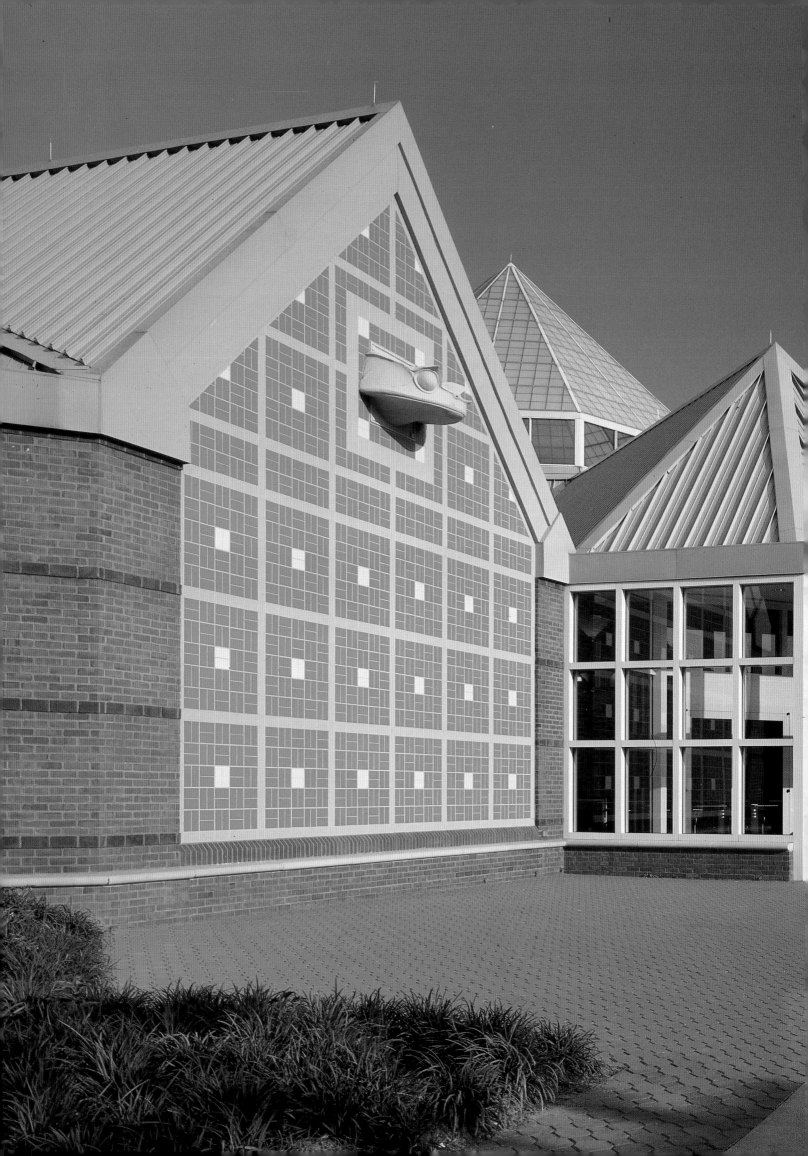

APPENDIX

ARCHITECTS

Anderson Mason Dale, P.C.
1615 17th Street
Denver, CO 80202
(303) 294-9448

Eugene Aubrey, FAIA
Pierce Goodwin Alexander & Linville
9805 Gulf Drive
Anna Maria, FL 34216
(813) 778-4300

Bradfield, Richards & Associates, Architects, Inc.
3025 Piedmont Road
Atlanta, GA 30305
(404) 231-5202

Brown Design Associates
(formerly Milkey & Brown)
66 Luckie Street-Suite 800
Atlanta, GA 30303
(404) 522-4310

Celli-Flynn and Associates
Architects and Planners
606 Liberty Avenue
Pittsburgh, PA 15222
(412) 281-9400

Cooke Douglas Farr Lemons/Ltd.
3780 I-55 North-Suite 101
Jackson, MS 39211
(601) 366-3110

CRSS Architects, Inc.
1177 West Loop South
Houston, TX 77027
(713) 559-2813

The Design Partnership
375 Fremont Street-Suite 200
San Francisco, CA 94105
(415) 777-3737

Di Marinisi & Wolfe
2 Park Plaza
Boston, MA 02116
(617) 451-5799

Dworsky Associates
3530 Wilshire Boulevard-Suite 1000
Los Angeles, CA 90010
(213) 380-9100

Gibson & Reno Architects
418 East Cooper Avenue-Suite 207
Aspen, CO 81611
(303) 925-5968

Hamilton Houston Lownie Architects, P.C.
172 Allen Street
Buffalo, NY 14201
(716) 885-0743

Hansen Lind Meyer
Drawer 310
Plaza Centre One
Iowa City, IA 52244
(319) 354-4700

Hansen Lind Meyer
800 North Magnolia Avenue-Suite 1110
Orlando, FL 32803
(407) 422-7061

Hellmuth, Obata & Kassabaum, Inc.
1831 Chestnut Street
St. Louis, MO 63130
(314) 421-2000

Hirsch Danois Architects, P.C.
246 West 38th Street
New York, NY 10018
(212) 302-6464

Hisaka & Associates
800 Euclid Avenue
Berkeley, CA 94709
(510) 525-3511

HKS Inc.
1111 Plaza of the Americas North, LB 307
Dallas, TX 75201
(214) 969-5599

Jova/Daniels/Busby
1389 Peachtree Street
Atlanta, GA 30309
(404) 892-2890

Kajima Corporation, Nagoya Office
2-14 Shinsakaemachi, Naka-Ku
Nagoya, Japan 460
0ll.81.52.961.6121 (From U.S.)

Kaplan McLaughlin Diaz
222 Vallejo Street
San Francisco, CA 94111
(415) 398-5191

Langdon Wilson Architecture Planning
3001 North Second Street
Phoenix, AZ 85012
(602) 241-0021

Llewellyn Davies-Sahni, Inc.
1900 Post Oak Boulevard
Houston, TX 77056
(713) 850-1500

Lord, Aeck & Sargent
1201 Peachtree Street, N.E.
400 Colony Square-Suite 300
Atlanta, GA 30361
(404) 872-0330

Albert C. Martin & Associates
811 West Seventh Street
Los Angeles, CA 90017
(213) 683-1900

Susan Maxman Architects
123 South 22nd Street
Philadelphia, PA 19103
(215) 977-8662

Midyette-Seieroe-Hartronft
3300 28th Street-Suite 200
Boulder, CO 80301
(303) 443-9960

Samuel Mockbee, FAIA
School of Architecture
Auburn University
Auburn, AL
(205) 844-4524

NBBJ
111 South Jackson Street
Seattle, WA 98104
(206) 223-5555

Nix, Mann and Associates, Inc.
1382 Peachtree Street, N.E.
Atlanta, GA 30309
(404) 873-2300

RNL Design
1225 17th Street-Suite 1700
Denver, CO 80202
(303) 295-1717

Rosser International, Inc.
524 West Peachtree Street
Atlanta, GA 30308
(404) 876-3800

Rothman Rothman Heineman Architects Inc.
711 Atlantic Avenue
Boston, MA 02111
(617) 451-6990

Shaughnessy Fickel & Scott Architects Inc.
920 Walnut
Kansas City, MO 64106
(816) 474-1397

Paul Silver, FAIA
Silver & Ziskind
233 Park Avenue South
New York, NY 10003
(212) 477-1900

The Stubbins Associates, Inc.
1033 Massachusetts Avenue
Cambridge, MA 02138
(617) 491-6450

Thompson, Ventulett, Stainback & Associates, Inc.
2700 Promenade Two
1230 Peachtree Street, N.E.
Atlanta, GA 30309
(404) 888-6600

TRO/The Ritchie Organization
3050 Bee Ridge Road-Suite A
Sarasota, FL 34239
(813) 923-4911

Turner Associates
57 Forsyth Street N.W.-Suite 1300
Atlanta, GA 30303
(404) 681-3214

Turner Associates/Architects & Planners, Inc.
55 Park Place, N.E.
Atlanta, GA 30303
(404) 681-3214

Voinovich-Monacelli Associates
1033 Massachusetts Avenue
Cambridge, MA 02138
(617) 661-1015

Voorsanger & Associates, Architects, P.C.
246 West 38th Street-14th Floor
New York, NY 10018
(212) 302-6464

Whitney Atwood Norcross Associates, Inc.
99 Chauncy Street
Boston, MA 02111
(617) 338-5446

Zimmer Gunsul Frasca Partnership
320 Southwest Oak-Suite 500
Portland, OR 97204
(503) 224-3860

David Miles Ziskind, AIA
Silver & Ziskind
233 Park Avenue South
New York, NY 10003
(212) 477-1900

PHOTOGRAPHERS

Joe C. Aker
4710 Lillian Street
Houston, TX 77007
(713) 862-6343

Tom Bernard
Tom Bernard Photography
586 Conestoga Road
Berwyn, PA 19312
(215) 296-9289

Tom Bonner
Tom Bonner Photography
1201 Washington Boulevard
Venice, CA 90291
(310) 396-7125

Doug Brown
P.O. Box 2205
Alexandria, VA 22301
(703) 684-8778

Jerry Butts
2046 Arapahoe
Denver, CO 80205
(303) 298-8837

Michael L. Christianer, AIA
Shaughnessy Fickel & Scott Architects Inc.
920 Walnut
Kansas City, MO 64106
(816) 474-1397

George Cott
2802 Azeele Street
Tampa, FL 33609
(813) 873-1374

Phil Eschbach
210 Chelton Circle
Winter Park, FL 32789
(407) 644-4539

Dan Forer
1970 Northeast 149th Street
North Miami, FL 33181
(305) 949-3131

Douglas R. Gilbert
138 State Street
Newburyport, MA 01950
(508) 465-8285

John Gillan
John Gillan Photography, Inc.
P.O. Box 164138
Miami, FL 33116
(305) 251-4784

Tom Hayes, AIA
Susan Maxman Architects
123 South 22nd Street
Philadelphia, PA 19103
(215) 977-8662

Biff Henrich
P.O. Box 111
Buffalo, NY 14222
(716) 884-5320

Ed Hershberger
7835 Southwest 34th
Portland, OR 97219
(503) 245-4158

David Hewitt/Anne Garrison
Architectural Photography
2387 Seaside Street
San Diego, CA 92107
(619) 222-4036

Jonathan Hillyer
Jonathan Hillyer Photography, Inc.
2604 Parkside Drive, N.E.
Atlanta, GA 30305
(404) 841-6679

Greg Hursley
4003 Cloudy Ridge Road
Austin, TX 78734
(512) 266-1391

Timothy Hursley
1911 West Markham
Little Rock, AR 72205
(501) 372-0640

Christopher Irion
183 Shipley Street
San Francisco, CA 94107
(415) 896-0752

Jeffrey Jacobs
Memphis, TN
(address and telephone number not available)

Edward Jacoby
108 Mount Vernon Street
Boston, MA 02108
(617) 723-4896

Phillip James
2300 Hazelwood Drive
St. Paul, MN 55109
(612) 777-2303

Balthazar Korab
P.O. Box 895
Troy, MI 48099
(313) 641-8881

Andrew Kramer, AIA
3600 Buckeye Court
Boulder, CO 80304
(303) 449-2280

Jane Lidz
433 Baden Hill
San Francisco, CA 94131
(415) 587-3377

Thorny Lieberman
Nathaniel Lieberman Studio
3648 Hazelwood Court
Boulder, CO 80304
(303) 443-1309

Mark Lohman
1021 South Fairfax
Los Angeles, CA 90019
(213) 471-3675

Susan A. Maxman, FAIA
Susan Maxman Architects
123 South 22nd Street
Philadelphia, PA 19103
(215) 977-8662

Robert E. Mikrut
63 Clinton Street
Newport, RI 02840
(401) 846-2134

John O'Hagan
Oxmoor House
2100 Lakeshore Drive
Birmingham, AL 35209
(205) 877-6201

Bob Pettus
6 Daniel Road
St. Louis, MO 63124
(314) 968-8631

Robert Reynolds
5331 Southwest Macadam
Portland, OR 97201
(503) 228-1859

James S. Roof
James S. Roof Photography
3855 Bridlewood Drive
Duluth, GA 30136
(404) 476-8553

Steve Rosenthal
59 Maple Street
Auburndale, MA 02166
(617) 244-2986

Shinkenchiku-Sha Co., Ltd.
2-31-2 Yushima
Bunkyo-Ku Tokyo Japan 113
011.03.3811.7101 (From U.S.)

Robert W. Springate
(address and telephone number not available)

Strode Eckert Photography
2136 Southeast Seventh Avenue
Portland, OR 97214
(503) 234-2344

Tod Swiecichowski
Switch, Inc.
205 Rice Street
Little Rock, AR 72205
(501) 372-6071

Mel Victor
Mel Victor Architectural Photography
5414 Northwest 79th Avenue
Miami, FL 33166
(305) 592-0884

Paul Warchol
133 Mulberry Street
New York, NY 10013
(212) 431-3461

Jean and John Williams
2172 North Landing Way
Marietta, GA 30066
(404) 591-5523

INDEX